Telling It Like It Was

Preaching In The First Person

David G. Rogne

CSS Publishing Company, Inc., Lima, Ohio

TELLING IT LIKE IT WAS

Copyright © 2001 by
CSS Publishing Company, Inc.
Lima, Ohio

All rights reserved. No part of this publication may be reproduced in any manner whatsoever without the prior permission of the publisher, except in the case of brief quotations embodied in critical articles and reviews. Inquiries should be addressed to: Permissions, CSS Publishing Company, Inc., P.O. Box 4503, Lima, Ohio 45802-4503.

Some scripture quotations are from the R*evised Standard Version of the Bible*, copyrighted 1946, 1952 ©, 1971, 1973, by the Division of Christian Education of the National Council of the Churches of Christ in the USA. Used by permission.

Some scripture quotations are from the *New Revised Standard Version of the Bible*, copyright 1989 by the Division of Christian Education of the National Council of the Churches of Christ in the USA. Used by permission.

Library of Congress Cataloging-in-Publication Data

Rogne, David George, 1934-
   Telling it like it was : preaching in the first person / David G. Rogne.
     p. cm.
   ISBN 0-7880-1794-2 (pbk. : alk. paper)
   1. Monologue sermons. 2. Biographical preaching. 3. Bible—Biography—Sermons. 4. Christian biography—Sermons. 5. Sermons, American—20th century. I. Title.
BV4307.M6 R64 2001
252—dc20   00-046842
                                                                                                                                                 CIP

For more information about CSS Publishing Company resources, visit our website at www.csspub.com.

ISBN 1-7880-1794-2   PRINTED IN U.S.A.

This is for Mary Jane
Sine Qua Non

Table Of Contents

Introduction	7
Chapter One Pharaoh And The Plagues	13
Chapter Two Solomon On Affluence	19
Chapter Three It's Love That Saves Us	27
Chapter Four Mordecai	35
Chapter Five Herod	43
Chapter Six John The Baptist	49
Chapter Seven The Betrayer	57
Chapter Eight Pilate's Story	65
Chapter Nine Francis Of Assisi	73
Chapter Ten A Man Of Integrity	81
Chapter Eleven A Reverence For Life	91
Chapter Twelve Trail Markers	99

Introduction

People who gather for worship have a variety of needs. Some are going through crises or temptations, experiencing pain or doubt, having difficulties in their homes or in their business lives. They may feel that they are the only ones who have experienced such difficulties. They despair because they feel no one else has been similarly tried. It would be helpful for them to learn that others have faced equally challenging or even more challenging circumstances and found strength for their journeys.

Others have negative attitudes or are engaged in destructive conduct. If they could see the consequences of such attitudes and actions in the life of another, it might lead to an amendment of life.

Still others need to become aware that they have gifts to be used for the benefit of others. If they could become acquainted with others whom God has used to influence the church and the world they might gain understanding of their own unique gifts. Those who have shared their gifts and opportunities are the heroes of the faith or of the race — people who have impacted our lives, shaped our destiny, and help us to be hopeful about the race.

People with these kinds of needs populate our congregations. They hope that somehow the service of worship will touch them in a meaningful way. In Protestant worship it is the sermon, the spoken word, that seeks to connect the situations of the hearers with the spiritual resources to meet their needs. Unfortunately, the sermon may fail to capture the imagination of the individual in such a way that necessary information is communicated and appropriate action is motivated. What is needed is a style of preaching that will capture the interest of the individual hearers, inform them about a resource in Scripture or Christian tradition which may be helpful to them in dealing with their own circumstances, and then motivate them to deal with that material in a useful manner.

If people could be made aware that there have been others who have had problems similar to their own, and learn that those others have found either the solutions for their problems or the courage to live with them, such people might feel relieved or strengthened.

Sometimes, however, the advice of the Apostle Paul, for example, or the word of some Old Testament prophet is thought to be too remote to be relevant to the life of a modern person. For this reason, much that might be of help in the religious tradition of an individual is dismissed. A style of preaching designed to make the heroes of the faith come to life, and to address issues of their day which have contemporary relevance, would be helpful.

One proposal for interesting, informing, and motivating members of a congregation is for the preacher to assume the identity of the subject of the sermon. This may be called first person preaching. It is the intention of this book to demonstrate how various situations may be addressed by this dramatic, autobiographical method of preaching.

I became involved with this style of preaching one Christmas Eve when I delivered a dramatic reading titled "The Other Wise Man" by Henry Van Dyke. It was not a monologue, but I discovered that by changing voices and styles of speaking I could accommodate all the parts. The congregation was so enthusiastic about this that I began to look around for other material which could be presented in the form of a monologue. Discovering that there was not a great deal of material available that was appropriate for use in a Christian worship service, I began to experiment by telling some of the more familiar stories of the Bible from the point of view of a participant in the event. For example, I told about the Slaughter of the Innocents from the point of view of King Herod. Such presentations involve the study not only of Scripture, but also of biblical history, secular history, and often, theology.

Initially, I felt that this kind of preaching was most appropriate during those times of the Christian year which lend themselves to a certain degree of pageantry and drama — notably Lent, Easter, Advent, and Christmas. I soon discovered, however, that what I had hit upon was more than entertainment. Members of the congregation were "hearing" things for the first time in stories and incidents with which they had been familiar since childhood. It occurred to me, then, that first person preaching could be more than simply a novelty — it could be used to bring home a point, or several points, in the same way that traditional preaching intends to do, but with greater drama.

Often, a first person sermon develops as I deal with a particular text and then become interested in the context. I begin to see that the situation out of which the biblical author was writing has certain parallels with our own situation, and that if the author himself were called upon to tell of his experience, individuals in the congregation could make the connection for themselves.

My method of preparation now is to study the passage I wish to present, study commentaries and the approaches of other preachers to the passage, read articles on the character or situation in a good Bible dictionary, and read one or more books on the character, if a definite character has developed. I then study pertinent books in the fields of theology and biblical introduction to ascertain what critical scholarship is saying about the time, author, and situation. To all this one must add imagination. What might have been going on in the mind of the character? What are the factors which might have led to a certain action?

It is also important to speak truthfully. At the very least this means to avoid knowingly presenting inaccurate information. For example, I wanted to present a sermon on Solomon which would be based on the book of Ecclesiastes. The book of Ecclesiastes seems to make the claim for itself that it was written by King Solomon. Biblical scholarship disagrees. Therefore, one needs to be cautious about how much of the content of the book of Ecclesiastes is to be attributed to Solomon. I dealt with this by having Solomon point out that it was a person called Koheleth, or "the preacher," who wrote the book of Ecclesiastes, but that Koheleth based much of what he said on certain experiences of Solomon. Solomon may then speak about some of the passages written by Koheleth as a description of some of the events of Solomon's life. This is demonstrated in one of the chapters later in this book.

Similar preparation is involved in preparing a message based on a non-biblical person. Sacred and secular history is filled with persons — saints, clergy, laypersons, well-known and unknown — who have witnessed to faith and enduring values, sometimes throughout their whole lives, sometimes in one shining moment. About such people there is usually an abundance of material available in seminary libraries and in local public libraries.

As the materials begin to accumulate, I generally discover that there are several experiences or ideas which developed in the life of the character which are applicable to life today. These then become the key ideas which I try to have the character get across to those who are listening. The remaining incidents in the life of the individual become the connecting links, which help to explain how the character progressed in her or his thinking or developed one idea after another.

Sometimes it seems appropriate to have the character point out how his experience relates to people living today. At other times it seems sufficient to have the character simply say how he dealt with his particular situation, leaving the application to the individuals who hear it. This means that the preacher has to decide before the final writing whether he or she conceives of the character as speaking only in the character's own time, or whether the preacher conceives of the character as having died and returned to the present congregation with certain insights which the character has gained because, in the interval, he or she has continued to stay attuned to the unfolding human situation.

One must further decide whether the character has subsequently changed his or her point of view and whether the character is now able to comment with the benefit of more mature reflection, or whether the character still has the same point of view which is historically attributed to her or him. For example, Herod, whose story is included in a later chapter, is far more interesting as an individual if he continues to be violent, erratic, and devious as he tells his story, rather than to be a person who has come to see the error of his ways. The hearers then have to examine their own hearts to see if there are ways in which their attitudes are similar to those of Herod. Judas, on the other hand, whose story is also included in a later chapter, is more useful homiletically as a person who recognizes what he has done and seeks to help others avoid a similar act.

Similar considerations must be made with regard to non-biblical characters. In preparing a first person sermon on Albert

Schweitzer, for example, I was attempting to help the congregation to understand the importance of reverence for life. Rather than simply telling the story of Albert Schweitzer from his birth to a certain point in his life, I felt that it would be more appropriate to describe how the idea of reverence for life crystallized in his own mind, and then move backward in time using some of his personal experiences to illustrate how he was being prepared to develop this idea. It is frequently of value, therefore, to pick up the life of an individual at some high point, or toward the end of his or her life, when his or her ideas have been more fully developed, and then to move backward in time in an attempt to reveal how the character developed to that point.

What follows are twelve first-person sermons, each prefaced by considerations the author was taking into account as that message was being prepared. The sermons are from three historical periods with four sermons from each period. The Old Testament period is represented by messages from the Pharaoh of the plagues, Koheleth, Hosea, and Mordecai. The New Testament period is represented by Herod, John the Baptist, Pilate, and Judas. The post-biblical period is represented by Francis of Assisi, Thomas More, Albert Schweitzer, and Dag Hammerskjold.

Chapter One

How does one take an old and familiar story regarding supernatural events that took place centuries ago in a far-off land and give it relevance for hearers today? Reliance on miracle, as in the case of the plagues in Egypt, may make the story charming, but not necessarily useful to people today who would like to believe in *deus ex machina* but really don't expect to experience it.

Recounting the story of the plagues in Egypt from Pharaoh's perspective gives hearers the opportunity to learn about Moses as a hero of faith, but at the same time, they may be enabled to see how a strictly secular approach to the events of our lives prevents us from seeing that there is a moral order in the universe that is drawing us toward justice and equity.

One valuable lesson, which the events of this story might illustrate, is the danger in the all-too-human characteristic of hubris. Pharaoh's estimate of himself keeps him from recognizing that the God of the universe is on the side of justice and equity. Like so many secularists today, he is satisfied with an approach to life that makes no place for a spiritual dimension. It is useful, therefore, to have Pharaoh speak for himself in a manner that will lead a modern skeptic to identify with him, so that when Pharaoh finally questions where his skepticism has led him, the skeptical listener will have to do the same.

A one-sentence proposition for this sermon is: "God chooses the insignificant who recognize him, rather than the mighty who reject him."

Pharaoh And The Plagues

Exodus 5-11

I am called Horus, Beloved of Truth, Defender of Egypt, Binder of the Barbarians, Rich in Years, Great of Victory, king of Upper and Lower Egypt, Son of Re, Good God, king of the Southland. My name is Ramses. I am Pharaoh, absolute ruler of Egypt, possessor of great armies, wealthier than any other king. Yet it profits me nothing. I have everything and I cannot enjoy it.

Have you ever met a man who you knew in advance was going to take all the joy out of living? It has been my great misfortune to encounter such a man. His name is Moses. He is kind of a labor organizer, a leader of the riffraff in my kingdom. He claims to be spokesman for a god you cannot even see. I've about had my fill of him and his whole lot. I would have had him eliminated early on, but over the years I've learned that one should never make a martyr out of any reformer. But who could have known it would come to this?

The first time I met him he tried to impress me with a cheap magician's trick to get me to listen to his cause. Here in Egypt it is possible to take a cobra, and by pressing on its neck, to make it become rigid like a stick. When the snake is thrown down, the paralysis is ended and it looks like a stick has become a snake. Moses tried that on me. I showed him that my magicians could do the same thing. I decided to nip this movement in the bud. I announced that if the Hebrews had time to follow a magician around, perhaps they didn't have enough work to do, so I increased their load. Needless to say, that didn't make Moses too popular with his own people.

Eventually, he became a real nuisance. Everywhere I went, he was there saying, "Thus says the Lord, 'Let my people go.'" People, ha! You know what those people are that he talks about?

Nothing, that's what they are ... just slaves. And he wants *me*, a king, to submit to their demands.

It so happens that we have had a series of adversities recently in Egypt — natural disasters, you could call them. And do you know what? This Moses is trying to get us to believe that *he* brought them to pass. And he's got just about everyone in Egypt believing him, everyone but me. Let me tell you how it started.

I was building two treasure cities, Pithom and Ramses. The latter is named after me. I pressed the Hebrews into my service because I needed their manpower. Then Moses came, as I have said, and demanded in the name of his god that I let the Hebrews go out into the wilderness, a three-days' journey out, so they could sacrifice to their god. I could see through that right away; if they ever got three days' distance from Egypt, we'd never get them back. He said that if I refused, his god would turn the Nile into blood, by which he meant that it would become red. Well, that was nothing new; there had been other years, when the Nile had been particularly high, that it brought down a great deal of red earth and algae from higher up. It so happened that after Moses spoke, the Nile *did* turn red for a week, but our own magicians have been able to forecast the same thing in time past. The water was foul for a while and a lot of fish died, but I was not impressed. I said: "No release."

Then, this Moses came again and said, "Let my people go, or there will be an invasion of frogs." I said, "No." And just as sure as you are sitting there, the next day frogs began to come out of the Nile in numbers you wouldn't believe. We've always had frogs along the bank, and they were never a bother. I assume that the unusually high river had given them an abundance of breeding places. There were hopping, croaking frogs everywhere — in houses, in beds, in closets, in pots and pans. That would have been tolerable, but after a few days they began to die. It probably had something to do with the dead fish I mentioned. Well, I thought, "It's just magic, but if Moses can get these frogs back into the river, at least we can get rid of the smell." I told him that if he would get rid of the frogs, I'd let his people go. The next day the live frogs were gone, but my magicians assured me that the frogs had just about run their course anyway, so I told Moses that I owed him nothing. Besides, the land was still covered with stacks of foul-smelling dead frogs!

Before long we had an infestation of mosquitoes. Mosquitoes are not uncommon here, but this was a particularly bad infestation, probably intensified by the abundance of breeding places left exposed by the unusually high river. But Moses claimed the credit for this, too. By this time he had completely confounded my magicians, and they were willing to admit that this must be in the hands of Moses' god. I held my ground, and in time the mosquitoes disappeared.

Moses met me at the river one day and said, "Let my people go, or there will be flies all over the land." I have to admit, he was a shrewd observer. With all these stinking frogs piled up all over the place, what else would you expect but flies? And sure enough, they came — little tropical, biting flies that breed well in upper Egypt, but not at all well down in the Mediterranean climate of Goshen, where the Hebrews live. So it looked like Moses' god was *favoring* the Hebrews, and *punishing* the Egyptians. I figured I'd get rid of this "I told-you-so" by granting his request. I said, "All right go, sacrifice to your god, but do it here in Egypt." I wasn't about to let them out of my sight.

I have to hand it to that Moses; he always has a reason for not compromising. He said, "No, that won't do. If we sacrifice in the presence of the Egyptians they will be offended by our mode of worship and stone us." Moses was probably right about that, so I said, "All right, just a little bit over the border, but get rid of these flies." He got rid of the flies, but then insisted on going a on three-days-journey away, and I refused.

As the waters receded, we were in for more trouble. Many of our farmers in upper Egypt let their cattle out to graze too soon after the flooding, and whatever had killed the fish and frogs, was still on the ground. Moses came and said that if I did not let the Hebrews go, there would be a plague on our animals. Sure enough, our animals began to die. But down in Goshen, where the waters receded more slowly, and the animals were stabled longer, they were not contaminated. My people could not see these connections, but I could, and so I refused Moses' request.

Moses, on the other hand, claimed he would extend the plague to people as well as to beasts. Many of my people broke out in boils and sores, particularly on their legs. I'm sure it had something to do with the biting flies which we had experienced earlier, but my people did not think so. My magicians were themselves suffering with the disease, and they were pleading with me to give in to Moses. He had beat them at their own game. But he did not convince me, and eventually the plague subsided.

Moses warned one day that there would be a terrible hailstorm unless I let his people go. I did not pay much attention to him, but I did notice a ripple of disturbance among the people of my court. In fact, many of them hurried out to get their animals into sheltered places. Sure enough, the storm came with thunder and lightening and hail. I could no longer afford the kind of hold he had on the imaginations of my people, so I publicly asked him to speak to his god about stopping the hail. It was the only politically expedient thing to do. But being humiliated that way, I was not about to let the Hebrews get clear away from me. Besides, my treasure cities were not yet completed, so I turned down Moses' requests.

Then Moses came up with the threat of a locust invasion. By this time he had my people running cold. They listened to him in fear, and when Moses left my presence, my people were insistent that I capitulate. I called Moses back and said, "Go ahead, take all your men, and worship as far away as you like, but leave your women and children here." I knew that if the men went, holding their families would bring them back. Then, without waiting for an answer, I ended the interview. Naturally, Moses found the terms unacceptable, but I appeared to my people to have been reasonable.

The locusts came. Frankly, they were worse than I had expected. To this day I have not figured out how Moses knew they were coming. I was desperate. Whatever had not been destroyed by the hail was being eaten by the locusts. So once more I relied on Moses' magic. I said, "Get rid of the locusts and I will let you go." The locusts were blown away by a strong wind, and it appeared to me the worst was over, so I thought better of the agreement. Now was not the time to let the Hebrews go. I refused.

Without any warning darkness came upon the land. Periodically we have in our country a hot south wind from the Sahara, which brings with it an abundance of sand that completely blocks out the light of the sun. It is called "Khamsin." This was worse than any I had experienced. It was augmented by the red dust left by the receding Nile, and by the fact that the hail and locusts had made our fields into dust bowls. This had all the marks of Moses' work, so I called him to the palace and said, "Go ahead, all of you, men, women and children, and sacrifice wherever you wish; only leave your flocks and herds where they are." Wouldn't you know he'd have an answer? "No," he said, "we cannot leave the animals. We will have to sacrifice from them, and we won't know how many we will need until we get where we are going." Well, I had had enough. It was obvious now that they had no intention of returning if I ever let them go. I told Moses to get out, and never to come before me again.

I have not seen Moses since. But my soldiers tell me he has given an ultimatum. If I don't let the Hebrews go, he says the first-born of our flocks and families will die. I don't suppose it is really true, but it certainly does make one stop and think. There really couldn't be such a god as Moses speaks of, could there? A god who demonstrates his power through the everyday occurrences of nature? A god who identifies himself with the cause of the downtrodden and the poor rather than with the powerful and the rich? A god who so inspires those who trust in him that they are confident that he will give them the victory? A god who is so strong that life and death itself are in his hands? Is there any god like that? The answer to that question may very well lead to the most important decision that I, or you for that matter, ever make.

Chapter Two

Some books of Scripture present us with quite a challenge if we wish to present our audience with a positive message. Certainly, one of the most challenging in this regard is the book of Ecclesiastes. I wanted to help my congregation become familiar with this book and its message, but the pessimism of the author seemed to provide little in the way of spiritual uplift. It occurred to me that Solomon, the purported author of the book, must have something that would be spiritually beneficial to my people. If Solomon's life could not provide us with a positive example of how to find the rewarding life, perhaps his life could show us some things to avoid.

I was aware from my Introduction to Old Testament course that it was not likely that Solomon wrote the book, at least not as it now stands. How, then, could we gain any moral instruction from his life based upon this book? I wanted to share with my congregation the benefits of biblical scholarship without becoming too technical. It occurred to me that this could be accomplished by having Solomon speak on his experiences using, in effect, the material which had been carefully gathered and organized by another, namely Koheleth, the preacher referred to in the opening of the book. The annual stewardship emphasis of the congregation provided a fitting opportunity for the presentation of the message that emerged.

Solomon On Affluence

I would like to tell you the story of a man who had everything, and show you how his abundance affected his life. It altered his relationships with others, his personal life, the life of his nation, and his religious outlook — all for the worse. *I* am that man — my name is Solomon — sometime king of Judah and Israel. I was not aware of what was happening at the time, but I am now well aware, and I should like to share some of my experiences with you so that, perhaps, what happened in my life can be avoided in yours. Do not say to yourself that our lives are so different that you can learn nothing from me, for my basic problem was one which people of every age are forced to live with. Much of what happened in my life was the result of my inability to cope with affluence — a newly found abundance of power, prestige, and wealth. Your own generation faces this problem and therefore, even though I am king, what happened in my life can happen in your life to a greater or lesser degree. In some ways it is easier to be upright when one is poor, for to live a godly life in the midst of wealth and power is not an easy thing to achieve.

In the book of Ecclesiastes there are some words that have been attributed to me, though they are really not my words. They are the words of a man who called himself Koheleth, or the Preacher. He used my life as an outline for what he wanted to teach. Much of what he said so accurately describes my experiences, that I will use his words where they apply.

The first thing that I want to do is to describe how affluence affected my relationships with others. I was born as the second son of Bathsheba and David the king. Their first son had died as an infant, so I was the oldest son of my father's favorite wife. But I had other half-brothers, one of whom, Adonijah, was older and in line for the throne. One day when my father was quite old and near death, Adonijah decided it was time for him to be anointed king. He called together all his supporters, including Abiathar, the high priest, and Joab, the commander of the army, and was preparing to have himself made king. My mother Bathsheba and Nathan, the prophet, heard about it, however, and they prevailed upon my father David to declare *me* to be king instead. My father agreed, and I was anointed king.

My brother and his supporters feared for their lives, so I assured them of amnesty. I believe I really meant it then, but as time went by I became more sensitive to their presence, more concerned to secure my position, more concerned to keep what I had inherited, and these people were a threat to me. One by one, I had them disposed of. But before you judge me too harshly, permit me to ask whether *you* have ever been elevated in position, and if so, did you not come to fear those under you? Did you not feel they were waiting for you to slip? Did you not breathe easier when they were gotten out of the way? Did you not wish you had the power to remove them? Oh, perhaps not to liquidate them, as I did, but to fire them, or get rid of them? Perhaps you have heard it said that power corrupts, and absolute power corrupts absolutely.

I began to learn how to use people. It was others who had brought me to power, not my own might or my abilities. Staying in power would also depend on how I used people. It becomes a question of what is more important: staying in control, or being seen by others as a nice person. I decided to stay in control. It is not without reason that Koheleth, writing in my name, should say, "Do not be surprised if you see the poor oppressed and justice and right violently taken away, for the high official is watched by a higher, and there are yet higher ones over them."

I must confess that I used women too. My first wife was the daughter of the king of Egypt. I loved her at first, and later built a special house for her. But it soon occurred to me how desirable it was to use marriage to ensure alliances. One alliance led to another and before it was over, I had accumulated 700 wives. Many of them were more political hostages than anything else. There could, of course, be no deep relationships with so many women, and I dealt with them as less than persons. In fact, I even acquired some 300 concubines.

It never occurred to me that women were persons, or that they needed fulfillment, or satisfaction, or tenderness — they existed for my benefit only. Do not laugh and say that the sheer enormity of my harem destroys any relevance between my situation and yours, for though we differ in number, we may agree in attitude, and it is there that the problem lies. The more affluent we become, the more preoccupied we become with our own enjoyment and pleasure. We become more and more concerned with ourselves and whether we are really getting all we feel entitled to, especially since we are now in a position to buy what we want. A man begins to ask himself whether any one woman is really capable of meeting all of his needs, and when he begins looking around, he is really no different from me. He has begun to consider other people as things which exist only for his own benefit. That is how affluence can affect our relationships.

The second thing I want to do is to describe how affluence affected me personally. To be sure, it adversely affected my character. Part of the problem was that I had been born with a silver spoon in my mouth. David, my father, had come up through the ranks. He had had to live by his wits; it molded his personality and led him to realize how much he depended upon God. Therefore, when he put pen to paper, in spite of his hardships and trials, he could still say, "Shout, rejoice, sing, praise God." But I had never known those hardships. I, too, felt a person should rejoice, but I couldn't bring myself to it. I had no knowledge of what I had been spared, no contrast to teach me how blessed I was. Saul had been a king after the people's heart. David had been a king after God's heart. I decided to be a king after my own heart. "Eat, drink, and be merry," said I. "The good and the bad have the same fate, so make the most of life." "The good man dies and the wicked man is praised in the city," so it occurred to me that it is not important how one conducts himself, just so he enjoys himself. I became a pursuer of pleasure, just as Koheleth described it in his writings. I cheered my body with wine; I erected great buildings; I built fine houses; I ate gourmet foods; I put in swimming pools; I was well entertained. I surrounded myself with material abundance and lived in such splendor that when the queen of Sheba came from the South to visit me she had to confess that in all the courts of the East she had not seen such splendor. Koheleth caught my attitude when he said, "Bread is made for laughter, and wine gladdens life, and money answers everything."

Oh, yes, I made a good impression, surrounded as I was with gold and silk and ivory, but where was the satisfaction I sought? Well did Koheleth express my thought when he said, "Sweet is the sleep of the laborer, whether he eats much or little, but the surfeit of the rich man will not let him sleep." I had everything, but I enjoyed nothing. I made no effort to control myself, and eventually everything became empty, useless, and vain. I came to see the pursuits and pleasures of humans as nothing more than striving after wind.

Has that never happened to you? You work hard to accumulate, you accomplish your goals, and you find that you have run out of challenges. You begin asking, "What is life all about anyway? Where is the meaning I thought I would find?" Ah, you may not have lived as unbridled a life as I, but I am sure that you have enough of the good things of life to know what I am talking about. You can enjoy only so many suits, only so many pairs of shoes; you can eat only one meal at a time, and when you have these things in abundance you begin to ask, "Where will I find the fulfillment that eludes me?"

I also turned my attentions to the pleasures of the mind, and I must say that affluence also had its effect on my mental powers. Some of my courtiers called me the wisest of men. In fact, that was the reason the queen of Sheba and many others made their state visits. The wisdom was a gift — a gift from God. When I first came to the throne I was young and inexperienced. I prayed that God would grant me the wisdom to rule well, and he answered my prayer. I had discernment and the power of good judgment to settle issues among my people. I was a student of nature, and I wrote treatises on botany and biology; I made proverbs and wrote wise sayings. But as with any gift, the mind must be cultivated if it is to continue to develop. But cultivation calls for discipline, and that would detract from my other pursuits. So instead, I gave the *pretense* of wisdom. I was the life of the party. I entertained with my witticisms and well-worn observations, but my powers of reason began to decline, until ultimately even wisdom gave me no pleasure. I think Koheleth put it well when he said, "Wiseman and fool alike come to the same end. Vanity, vanity, all is vanity."

The third thing I want to do is to describe how affluence affected my religious life. I had started my reign as a true seeker after God. You remember how I told you of my prayer for guidance. I did this humbly and earnestly, and God granted my desire. But that was religion in its simplest dimension, I thought. As I gained an appreciation for the finer things of life, it seemed reasonable that the worship of God should also become more elaborate. The old ways in which our ancestors worshiped seemed crude and primitive, so we laid plans for a temple. No longer would God be worshiped just anywhere. Worship would become regulated, at specified times and places. We would centralize for efficiency so that religion could keep pace with the times.

It took us seven years to build the Temple, but when it was completed I'm sure the people were pleased, even though it required heavy taxes and forced labor. It eventually took shape as the kind of house in which a first-rate nation would want its God to live: gold, ivory, fine woods, and elaborate craftsmanship. Now God was where we could find him when we needed him, and we had a first-class place in which to meet him.

But there was something unsatisfying in all this, too. We had God in a box. Instead of being a basic element of all of life, religion became something that was done at certain times and in a certain place. Religion was divorced from life — cut off from the action of day-to-day living. The more I was preoccupied with advancement and achievement and pleasure, the less time there was to consider the religious dimensions. And if I did not actually *go* to the Temple, the greater the chance that I would not think of God at all. In my attempt to make religion respectable, I had managed to make it impersonal. Small wonder, then, that I became interested in the bizarre religions of my foreign wives. I thought perhaps I would find in them the dimension I was missing in my own religion.

The problem was not that my God was not adequate for my needs, but that I had deprived him of any personal relationship in my life. Have you never encountered that problem? God becomes forced into respectable conformity, and your relationship to him becomes formal and cold? I think it is uniquely a problem for the affluent. They are prepared to accept only a respectable and sophisticated approach to God. Their religious expressions become formalized, stiff, and unsatisfying. Then, failing to find God personal and approachable, some people become irreligious or fall into despair.

That is what happened to me. I sought for meaning without God and found only futility. Again Koheleth caught my mood when he said, "I saw that under the sun the race is not to the swift, nor the battle to the strong, nor bread to the wise, nor riches to the intelligent, nor favor to men of skill, but time and chance happen to them all." Nothing rules the world but chance: you will one day be caught in the net like a fish; and when you are dead that will be the end.

It was that very despair which I could not ultimately buy. Death comes to all living things, but humans cry out for the eternal. There was a time when in my heart I said with Koheleth, "The fate of the sons of men and the fate of beasts is the same; as one dies so dies the other. They all have the same breath, and humans have no advantage over the beasts; for all is vanity." Have you ever felt that way? I am afraid none of us is exempt from such thoughts, and occasionally they lead to despair. What word of hope, then, amid this crushing gloom?

For me, it was the concept of justice. I could not accept a world view in which there was no justice. And if justice, then an eternal dimension to life, for there must be a place for the balancing of the books, if not here, then hereafter. And if there is an eternity, then it matters how one lives, and I had been living all wrong. All my privileges, all my opportunities had been spent on myself, and it brought me only to despair. Obviously, that kind of life was not what God intended.

I was now old, and my life was far spent. It had been spent on myself, and I had been unhappy. I could not go back and make up the error of my living, but I could at least pass on my experience. Therefore, the sum of all I have recounted is what I give you now, in the words of Koheleth: "Remember your creator in the days of your youth, before the evil days come, and the years draw nigh, when you will say in your heart, 'I have no pleasure in them.' " If God has blessed you with affluence, rejoice in it, but remember that you are also responsible to him for how you use it: "Rejoice, O young man, in your youth, and let your heart cheer you in the days of your youth; walk in the ways of your heart and the sight of your eyes. But know that for all these things God will bring you to give an accounting."

Chapter Three

Old Testament prophets are often depicted as stern preachers of doom. As we read their warnings, it is easy to forget that they were human beings like ourselves. We forget that their preaching arose out of their experiences and observations. When the Lectionary presented the opportunity to preach on a text in Hosea, it occurred to me that this would be a good time to show how our personal experience and our reflection on those experiences shape our theology.

Old Testament introductions and commentaries make it clear that there is difference of opinion regarding the sequence of events that unfold in Hosea's description of his relationship with his wife Gomer. I felt that the suggested sequence in which Gomer leaves the marriage relationship strengthened the significance of the subsequent restoration. Allowing Hosea to share his own story allows us to feel his vulnerability and to gain an appreciation for what God feels when we reject the relationship he offers us.

My objective in this sermon was to help people understand the depth of God's love for humankind. A one-sentence proposition of its message would be: "As Hosea came to understand his love for his erring wife, he came to understand God's love for an erring people."

It's Love That Saves Us

Hosea 1-3; 11:1-9

Have you ever wondered how it is that a person gets inspired with ideas about God? Certainly, a lot of what we believe about God comes to us from people of the past who had certain experiences. Moses, for example, that great man of God, was a channel through whom God communicated the idea that there are certain laws of conduct that one must follow if life is to be satisfying. From Moses, therefore, we picked up the idea that God is the great lawgiver.

Later, the Psalmists, reflecting on those laws, tended to see God as a rewarder of the good. They reminded us that "the steadfast love of the Lord is from everlasting to everlasting upon those who fear him, and his righteousness to children's children, to those who keep his covenant and remember to do his commandments." It was from such writings that we Jews got the idea, rightly or wrongly, that God loves only those who are good.

There were also the prophets, stern men like Amos, who preached on the justice and severity of God. They caused us to see that God is a righteous judge of conduct, and woe to us if our conduct was not upright. Through Amos, we learned to fear the Lord. Sometimes those prophets of unrelieved doom gave us the idea that God was cold, indifferent, impatient with our human frailties. I suppose you could say that I generally fell into that school, too, at least in the early days of my preaching. My name is Hosea. Like Amos, my predecessor, I was called to be a prophet, a preacher, a spokesman for God. The only God I knew about was the stern God preached by Amos. So I preached that my people were heading straight for destruction — going to hell in a handbasket, you might say — and from all I could see, if that was what they got, it served them right. At least, that's the way I went about my preaching at first.

But something happened in my own life which was to have a profound effect on the way I understood God. That is why I asked you at the beginning how you think a person gets inspired with ideas about God. You probably think that God speaks directly to certain people, word for word, the things that God wants them to say, and those people pass the words on to the rest of us. Maybe God does do that sometimes. I can't speak for Moses, but I'll bet that a lot of what Moses had to say came to him as God helped him try to make sense out of the situation in which he found himself. Then the words were written down for our benefit, and our understanding of God was increased.

As a preacher, I felt it was my task to pass on the ideas and warnings from the past, to preach judgment and condemnation. I wasn't changing anybody. I wasn't making anybody happy by what I said, but I felt that that is what a preacher does. Give 'em hell! At least keep 'em from enjoying what they are doing! Then God spoke to me. Not in words you could hear, but through my experience. In my case, it was through my marriage that God made me aware of some things about which I had formerly been ignorant.

The first thing I had to learn about God deals with our relationship to him. I was a happily married man. My wife's name was Gomer. She bore me three children and I thought that everything was just fine in our marriage; the rent was paid, we were clothed and fed, I had work, everybody was healthy. I don't know quite what happened between us; maybe I spent too much time being a preacher, and not enough time being husband and father. You know, it's one of the hazards of being a preacher that you are always on call. Maybe Gomer couldn't handle it. Maybe I brought too much of my work home. I know I was terribly intense. I felt that it was my job to denounce the sins of the people, and there was plenty to denounce. The people were greedy, materialistic, self-indulgent, and, therefore, taking advantage of others. The religious establishment was corrupt. The government officials were seeking bribes and corrupting justice. I felt that they needed to be convicted of their sins.

You probably know that preachers are always looking for illustrations to help them make their point. Perhaps you have heard preachers use illustrations based on experiences in their homes or with their children. Well, I thought I would go one better. People weren't paying any particular attention to what I said, so I decided that instead of speaking of my children in sermons, I would work it so that wherever my children went, they would be a constant reminder of God's judgment. As the father, I had the right to name the children. My first child I named Jezreel. This was a place of bloody battles in Israel's history. It was kind of like naming a child Armageddon. Wherever he went, when people asked his name, the name would serve as a warning that a day of reckoning was coming for the people of Israel.

My second child, a girl, I named Lo-ruhamah, which means "not pitied." Wherever she went, her name would be a living message that divine judgment was about to fall on Israel without pity. My third child, a son, I named Lo-ammi, which means "not my people." I wanted the people of Israel to know that whatever covenant they thought they had with God was broken. Israel could not expect to continue to enjoy a preferred status under God's protection, for her very life denied that she was a people of God. I suppose that I made my point very well, but my methods and my message must have made our home a bitter and loveless place, for eventually, my wife left me.

In my misery, I thought to myself, "How like marriage is God's relationship with his people." God had called Israel when she was but a wandering group of tribes in the wilderness. God gave her continuity, purpose, leadership, protection, food, a homeland. It was God who made Israel what she was. God had entered into a covenant akin to marriage: Israel was to be true to God, and God was to care for Israel. Israel freely consented to the agreement at Mount Sinai, but corruption soon set in. God had attempted to refine the covenant through the law, the prophets, the priests, the religious ceremonies, but without success. Injustice, oppression, and exploitation continued to be a part of Israel's pattern, so that she became less and less what God had intended her to be.

Of course, I identified *myself* with God's position in my relationship with Gomer. I was angry. I had provided her with a place to live, a family, the necessities of life. She should have been grateful. As far as I was concerned, Israel and Gomer had each chosen to go their own way, and both should be permitted to follow their course to destruction, if that is where it led. God would be justified, and so would I!

The second thing I had to learn, however, was the pain of alienation. Not only did Gomer leave me, she went off and became a prostitute. There was abroad in our land the abominable practice of Baal worship. The Baals were fertility gods who were believed to provide for the increase of flocks and herds and crops. The people thought of Baal as husband of the land and people, and they thought of his union with them as one based on marriage and sexual union. This was accomplished by entering into sensuous and immoral rites with women who were in attendance at the shrines. Gomer had become one of these women. She got her support, her food, her lodging, from those who became her lovers. She was reduced to seeking only the physical necessities: food, drink, and clothing. She had given up any consideration of those things which went deeper than physical need; she was not concerned for love or affection or responsibility. She was utterly alienated from me.

And yet, I could not forget her. A part of me said, "Let her go. Good riddance! She has freely chosen this way for herself. Have nothing to do with her!" I was bitter; I was disappointed; I was hurt. But I was also tormented by my separation from her. I didn't want to love her. I felt degraded by her. But I loved her nevertheless, this faithless one who did not deserve my love, and I desperately wanted her back.

Here was the turning point in my understanding of God. I began to see beyond my own pain to the pain of God. If *my* love for faithless Gomer could still endure, how much more the love of God for God's erring people. How many times had Israel gone off after its Baals, violating its agreement to be God's people, and entering into unholy alliances which must have torn the heart of God? How many times had Israel attributed its increase, its flocks, its herds, its advancement to Baal rather than to God who was the real provider? Israel so often acted like a confused wife, going after those things she thought would bring happiness and security, only to find that the pursuit of physical goals left her empty and unfulfilled.

Realizing all this, my message changed. I felt God was telling me, "Continue loving Gomer; you are allowed to love her, you must love her, for even so do *I* love Israel." My longing to have my own wife back was but a symbol of the longing God feels for his estranged people. I, who sat alone in the ruins of my own broken home, was given a vision of God, not as a judge, enraged by broken laws, but as a lover, alone, with his head in his hands, brokenhearted by desertion. I could hear God saying, "How shall I give you up? How shall I deliver you, O Israel?"

But I found more than suffering; I found also the possibility of reconciliation. Things had gone badly for Gomer. When she was no longer of value to the shrine of Baal, she had been ejected. Having nowhere to go, she wound up in debt and was eventually sold to a slave dealer. She was now owned by the way of life she had sought to follow. No longer was she free to choose her way of life.

Such was her condition when I found her: a poor miserable thing to be bought and sold in the market place. I paid the price for her so that she was released from bondage. There was no need for the punishment I had so long preached as the payment for sin. Gomer had known punishment enough: the degradation of chasing false lovers; the poverty of goods and spirit which were the result of her slavery; the drabness that had come into her life from the pursuit of pleasure. What Gomer needed now was knowledge that she was a person of worth, for she had lost her dignity. She needed to know she could be loved, for she was no longer able to love herself. In short, she needed to be redeemed, not scolded. I brought her back to our home and asked her to be my wife again. I did not expect fawning gratitude from her; neither do I expect admiration from you. In those long months without her, I had discovered that *I* was as responsible for what had happened as was she. My own attitudes had to change. No condescension. No blaming. I sought her and wooed her again because I loved her and needed her. She was helping me to understand the meaning of love.

In all this I saw hope for God's people. God does not stand idly by when his people have spurned his love. He absorbs the pain and seeks them out nonetheless. His victory is not found in our destruction, but in our redemption. God so loves the world that he only wins when we are redeemed, won back to him. He is with us, no matter how far we have fallen. He comes among us, he suffers with us, he takes the initiative in rescuing us, not because of any merit in us, but simply because he loves us.

And how this realization changed my message! I changed the name of my daughter, Lo-ruhamah, "not pitied," to Ruhamah, meaning "she has obtained pity." I changed the name of my son, Lo-ammi, "not my people," to Ammi, meaning "my people." I had discovered that God was wooing his people back to himself. My message was no longer the negative one of judgment and punishment, but the good news that we who had been alienated from God were still loved by God and could be reconciled to God once again. And this good news of God's love is not simply for Israel; it is for all people. God loves *us* and seeks *us* to be his people even now.

Chapter Four

Certainly there are many stories in Scripture which should be presented from the perspective of the female involved. A case in point is the story of Esther. But how to present her story in the first person if the presenter is male? It is difficult for a male to stand before a congregation and say: "My name is Esther." Fortunately, Esther's story is closely tied to that of her kinsman, Mordecai. It works out well to have him tell her story from his point of view.

I wanted to do more than simply acquaint people with the story of Esther. While one could claim that simply familiarizing people with the contents of the Bible is an adequate goal for preaching, I feel that preaching ought to apply the lessons learned from Scripture. In this story Esther becomes an example of a person who seizes her opportunity. That is a lesson for all of us to learn. My objective was to show how God can operate in human life when a person cooperates with him. My one-sentence proposition is: "God is at work in the world for justice, but God requires the cooperation of individuals."

Mordecai

Esther 4:10-16

About 400 years after David had been made king of Israel, Nebuchadnezzar, king of Babylon, laid siege to the city of Jerusalem. A year later he captured the city, and in reprisal took many of Judah's chief citizens into captivity in Babylon. In 586 and again in 581, the residents of Judah revolted and both times, when the revolts were put down, more people were deported to Babylon where they stayed for seventy years or more.

Later in the same century Cyrus, king of the Medes and Persians, conquered Babylon and permitted those Jews who wished to do so to return to Judah. By that time, however, many Jews had become comfortable in their new surroundings — and some even moved farther into Persia. My ancestors were among the latter group. As a result of that migration, I happened to live in Susa, one of the five capital cities of Persia, in the days when Ahasuerus, the king of Persia, came to power. My name is Mordecai, a simple Jew, who, by the grace of God, became prime minister of all Persia and second only to the king himself.

I would like to share my story with you as an illustration of God's providential care, in hopes that you will be able to see God at work in your life as he was in mine. I must concede that my story is largely tied up with that of Esther, who was one day to save her people.

I suppose the first thing I should talk about is God's preparation for the deliverance he was later to accomplish. It started near the beginning of Ahasuerus' reign. It took him several years after he assumed the title "king" to become ruler-in-fact, putting down rebellious elements and consolidating the empire. When that was accomplished, in the third year of his reign, the king called for a coronation celebration in Susa which was to last six months. Governors, princes, and generals from 127 provinces stretching all the way from Ethiopia to India were invited.

As the celebration was drawing to a close, the king authorized one final banquet which was to last seven days. The king and his male guests had been drinking for several days and they were in a pretty sorry state. The queen, Vashti, had been entertaining the wives of the nobility in a different part of the palace and they were in a more sober state. In his drunkenness, the king sent word demanding that Vashti appear before his guests so that he might show off her beauty. The queen refused to come into such a drunken situation, and the king became enraged. We did not know it then, but at that moment the stage was being set for the deliverance of the people of Israel from a danger which had not yet come to the surface.

The king called in his wisemen and asked what should be done to Queen Vashti, who had not performed the command of the king. The wisemen counseled that if the queen's insubordination went unpunished, wives all over the empire would look with contempt on the authority of their husbands and there would be domestic chaos. Therefore, their advice was that Vashti be deposed and a new queen be put in her place, so that women would recognize that every man is lord of his own house. The king agreed, and Vashti was deposed.

In time the king began to wonder whether he had done the right thing. But it was too late to reinstate Vashti because the king had issued a proclamation against her, and the proclamation of a Persian king may not be altered. Therefore, the king's wisemen quickly counseled that young women be brought from all over the empire so that the king might choose from among them one to be his queen. This pleased the king, and he issued such a decree.

It was at this point that Esther and I entered the picture. Esther was my younger cousin, orphaned child of my uncle. I had raised her as my own daughter and she had developed into a beautiful young woman. When I encouraged Esther to take her chances in the competition, she consented. I told her not to mention her nationality or her relationship to me lest being a member of a minority group should work against her. That little secret was eventually to be an asset, for Esther won the heart of the king and he made her his queen.

I held a minor government position in those days, which required that I sit at the gate of the palace each day to do business. One day while I was there I chanced to hear two palace guards plotting to assassinate the king. I got word to Esther as quickly as I could, and she in turn informed the king in my name, though not mentioning our relationship. The matter was investigated and found to be true, and when the two guards were judged, my name was written in the book of the king's Chronicles as a benefactor of the king. The stage was set for a great drama.

If the first thing that needed to be mentioned was God's preparations, I suppose the next thing that needs to be mentioned is human prejudice. In those days, the king needed a prime minister, and the man chosen for the job was Haman the Amalekite. He was an evil man, consumed with ambition and pride. He exulted in the fawning obeisance, the bowing and scraping before him, which went with his position, and everybody did it. Everybody except me. I refused to bow before his new-found power and authority because I could not respect him as a man.

When my refusal to bow as he passed by became known to him, he was consumed with anger and determined to destroy me. But he was not content to lay hands on me only. Someone told him that I was a Jew, and he began to make plans for the destruction of all the Jews in the Persian Empire. That is how prejudice develops, isn't it? Someone takes the characteristics of one person he doesn't like, whether rightly or wrongly, and he transfers those characteristics to a whole race, so that he can justify his hatred.

Bit by bit, Haman put his plan together. He consulted oracles who threw lots to determine an auspicious month and day on which to carry out his nefarious plot. The dice, called pur, hit upon the fourteenth of March, which was then some eleven months away. He then went to the king with his evil counsel. "There is a certain people scattered abroad throughout the kingdom," he said, "whose laws are different from every other people, and they do not keep the king's laws, so that it is not profitable to the king to tolerate them." He urged the king to issue a decree authorizing the destruction of the Jews. More than that, he offered to put 10,000 talents of silver in the king's treasury to cover expenses.

The king had no reason to question Haman's judgment, and the money helped to make it seem right, so without even asking who the people were who were to be treated so, the king gave Haman authority to write letters to all the provinces, authorizing the inhabitants to rise up on the fourteenth of March and slay, destroy, and annihilate all Jews, young and old, women and children, and to take the possessions of the Jews as plunder. There was not a strong feeling of anti-Semitism in the kingdom, but this decree pointed out that we Jews were different, and the promise of plunder quickly fanned the flames of hatred. Understandably, Jewish people everywhere were filled with fear and deeply distressed, as was I.

Because of human prejudice, the next thing that happened could be called the plan of Mordecai. It was quite simple, really. We needed a friend at court. I told Esther what had happened and charged her to go to the king and entreat him for her people. Esther protested that if anyone went to the king in the inner court without being called, there was but one law: all were put to death, except those to whom the king held out his scepter. She went on further to say that she had not been called in to see the king for thirty days. Knowing how capricious he was, to barge in on him could certainly mean death.

I nevertheless urged Esther that she must take advantage of the unique opportunity which was hers. God was capable of bringing deliverance in many ways, but woe to her to have the opportunity and not use it. I said, "Who knows but that you have been made queen for such a time as this."

I am convinced that things work that way in the lives of many of us. We are given opportunities to do the things God wants done. We just happen to be there at the right time, and woe to us if we do not take advantage of it. Esther was convinced. She said, "I will go to the king though it is against the law, and if I perish, I perish."

Esther handled things beautifully. She dressed herself in her finest gown and went before the king. When he saw her, he looked favorably on her and held out the golden scepter, saying, "What is it, Queen Esther? What is your request? It shall be given you, even to the half of my kingdom." Esther knew better than to press her luck. Instead she invited both the king and Haman to come to dinner that very day, which they both consented to do. At the dinner, the king asked again what her petition was, and again she deferred, requesting that the king and Haman come to dinner again the next day. They both agreed, and Haman went off joyfully and glad of heart.

So you begin to see the plan of Mordecai. What we see next is the pride of Haman. As I indicated, Haman was very satisfied with himself. He had property, wealth, family, power, the ear of the king, and now even inclusion in the activities of the queen. However, as he left the palace his eyes fell on me, and as I refused to bow, his countenance fell. I have been told that he went home that day and called together his friends and told them of his honored position and of the fact that he was to be honored again by being invited by the queen the next day also. Then he went on to tell his friends that, in spite of all these benefits, he could not enjoy them because whenever he saw me it took all his pleasure away.

His friends suggested that he have a gallows built right in his own courtyard, and that he go to the king early the next day and request permission to hang me from it so that he could go to the queen's dinner with a happy heart. The idea pleased Haman, and so sure was he of the king's permission that he had the gallows built at once. Someone should have told him that "pride goes before a fall."

It just so happened that during the course of the night the king could not sleep. Something was bothering him, but he couldn't bring it into focus, so he asked that the book of the king's Chronicles be read to him, so that he might see if there were something in it that he needed to do. In the course of reading, it was mentioned that one Mordecai had saved the king's life by reporting a plot. The king asked what honor had been bestowed on Mordecai for this, and it was reported that nothing had been done.

About this time, Haman came back to the palace, hoping to find the king still awake so that he could get the permission to hang me in the morning. But before Haman could make his request, the king asked him, "What shall be done to the man whom the king delights to honor?" Haman thought to himself, "Whom would the king delight to honor more than Haman?" So he advised the king to dress such a man in a royal robe, place him on the king's horse, and have the noblest prince lead the horse through the streets, saying, "Thus shall it be done to the man whom the king delights to honor." The idea pleased the king, and he ordered Haman to do just as he had said for Mordecai, who sat at the king's gate. Ah, what a crushing blow! Haman did it, but you should have seen him. A more unhappy person could not be imagined. He led me all through the streets on the king's horse. But I am informed that he went straight home in great mourning and told his friends what had happened. They were of no comfort to him, but instead told him that this was an omen of bad things to come.

If what I just related speaks of the pride of Haman, I suppose the final phase could be called the working out of the providence of God. The king and Haman came the second time to Esther's feast. This time, when the king asked for Esther's request, she answered, "My petition is that my life and the life of my people be given me, for we have been sold to destruction." The king was surprised and asked who had done this, to which Esther responded, "This wicked Haman!" The king rose in anger and went into the palace garden. When he returned he saw the terror-stricken Haman falling on the couch where Esther sat, begging for his life. It appeared that he was assaulting the queen, and the king was incensed. Seeing that things were going against Haman anyway, one of the guards, who did not like Haman, informed the king that Haman had also built a gallows from which to hang the man whom the king had just honored. That was all the king needed! He gave the command that Haman should be hung from it instead, for his evil intention and presumption.

Still, the important thing was not vengeance or the destruction of Haman, but to save the Jewish people. Esther revealed to the king that she and I were related, that we were Jews, and that it was the Jews whose destruction he had decreed. The king was filled with sorrow and sincerely wanted to revoke the order, but a royal decree could not be revoked. He called me in and told me to come up with an alternative statement and he would sign it. I, therefore, drew up a proclamation which said, in effect, that if any Jews were attacked on March fourteenth, the king urged them to defend themselves, and he put the weight of his favor on their side. Few people would be foolish enough to go against the favor of the king, even if the first decree permitted it. The princes, nobles, and generals were especially cautious. There was now gladness and joy among the Jews. In time, the king gave me his signet ring and elevated me to the position which had formerly been held by Haman.

When the fourteenth of March came, there were those who did attack the Jews; the prospect of plunder and the fanning of the flames of racial prejudice had found their willing instruments. But the Jews defended themselves well and were saved from wholesale slaughter. To this day, on March 14, we Jews celebrate the Festival of Purim, named after the dice which Haman threw, in commemoration of our great deliverance through the courage of Esther.

What I am trying to get across by the telling of my story is that there is such a thing as the providence of God. Why that providence is not always evident I do not know. We Jews have more reason to be realistic about the seeming inactivity of God than any other people I know, yet we believe. I do not suggest that we be Pollyanna and tell ourselves that what happens is always for the best, or that what happens is always the will of God. The truth is that people have something to say about what happens in the world, evil people and good people. Someone has said that all that is necessary for the triumph of evil is that good people do nothing. God has a will for the world, but he works through people, people who are in tune with his will and who have the courage to act on what they believe. That is what happened with Esther, who used her opportunity. Who knows what providential thing *you* might be responsible for, if you, too, will trust in God and remain alive to the opportunities God gives you.

Chapter Five

    The world is often cruel to children and other innocents. It did not end with Herod. The newspapers are filled with the evidence that the slaughter of the innocents still takes place today. We live in a world where might seems to make right. We may wonder what kind of person could give the order to destroy children. A closer look at king Herod may help us to see the characteristics that are abundantly in evidence in despots today. The basic characteristic is a self-obsession that crowds out every other allegiance.

    A good Bible dictionary provides sufficient background to fill in the details of Herod's life and help us to see that from the beginning he was a sociopath whose only concern was with his own advancement. Even as he speaks of himself and of all that he has had to do to get and maintain power, he casts a shadow which makes the qualities of Christ shine more brightly. As Herod attempts to convince us that he is uniquely qualified to be king, we are led to long for the reign of Christ. But it is not enough simply to assure ourselves that we would have chosen Christ if we had been there. Herod closes by challenging the hearers to examine their present conduct to see what it says about their loyalty.

Herod

Matthew 2:1-12

I suppose you've come here about that incident over in Bethlehem. Well, you've come to the right place. I'm King Herod. I gave the order. I admit it sounds bad at first. All those children killed by soldiers. But it was necessary! I had to protect the established order. You can't have rivals for the throne springing up all over the place. That leads to anarchy. A king has to take direct action; that discourages sedition. I've learned that from my years in politics.

Not just anybody can be king. Some people would make a terrible mess of things. I've had to protect the people from getting a bad king. After all, a child born in Bethlehem, what kind of influence could he have in the world? A king has to have certain qualifications if his reign is going to amount to anything.

For one thing, a king has to have connections. That's a subject that I know something about! My father, Antipater, was an Idumean. Not only was he not a Jew, but he was from a people who were occasionally enemies of Jews. He pulled himself up by his boot straps. At first he was a friend of the Roman general, Pompey. Then, when Pompey was defeated by Julius Caesar, my father became a friend of Caesar. In return, Caesar made my father a Roman citizen and prime minister in Palestine. I learned right then that it matters who you know, so when Caesar was murdered, and Cassius, one of his murderers, was on top, I sided with him.

Eventually, Mark Antony came to our country following Caesar's murder. Naturally, I cultivated *his* friendship and, out of gratitude, he made me military governor in Syria. Of course, one does not get power for nothing. I had to make it financially worthwhile for Antony, for he was greatly in need of funds. And I had to pledge my support to him. But, alas, he got tied up with that Egyptian woman, Cleopatra, and after the battle of Actium it was all over for him.

Naturally, my support then went to Antony's successor, Octavius, who was now on top. I begged his forgiveness for having supported Antony, and he, being an understanding man, made me king of the Jews. Of course, it was harder to convince the Jews that I should be their king. But as you can see, I have managed well enough, largely because of my connections.

But what of this child born to peasants? What connections could he have? He might be a Jew, and therefore more acceptable to the Jews than I. But what could he ever amount to? I'm a Roman citizen. That gives me connections with the most powerful nation on earth. That is what a king needs. I am known to kings and generals. Palestine needs a man like me in control. I've got connections, and those I don't have I can afford to buy. What could *he* afford, being born a peasant? After all, when you know kings, who else is necessary?

So you see, it wasn't for myself that I gave the order to kill those children. It was to protect Palestine from an individual who, in years to come, might take seriously the things that others were saying about him and offer himself as a king. He might have caused the people to make an unwise choice. Connections — that is what a king must have.

The second qualification a king needs is to be a realist. I dare say, if I am anything, I am a realist! You've probably heard some of my enemies criticize the fact I've had ten wives. I don't deny it, but I need to point out that some of those marriages were for the good of the state. Doris, my first wife, had no background at all — no family, no wealth. She really wasn't a proper wife for a king.

My second wife, Mariamne I, was the love of my life. Not only that, she came from an influential family. Her older brother was the one the Jews really looked to as the legitimate heir to the Jewish throne. I pointed out to Antony the problem of having that young man around if we were to bring peace to the land, and Antony wisely had the matter taken care of.

Of course, that meant that any son born to Mariamne could be a king, since she was next oldest in that family. So I married her in order to identify myself with any legal heir. She did have a younger brother, about seventeen years old, who could have upset things if the people ever rallied to his support. One day he went bathing with some of my men, and the poor fellow drowned in the bathing pool. Mariamne blamed me for that, and things were never the same between us. I had a hard time with that family from then on. There were 45 prominent Sadducees who had supported her brother's claim. I had them rounded up because they were dangerous to the state. They could make the Romans think that all was not well under my rule. A king has to protect his people from dangerous elements, so they were gotten rid of. My relationship to Mariamne became increasingly strained after that until one day she provoked me, and while I didn't mean to, in a fit of anger I killed her.

There were some other marriages. I married two of my nieces to keep their heirs in the family. You must understand that I always had the kingdom in mind. My marriages were to provide heirs so that the Romans would not have to come in and rule again.

You might ask, were there no heirs by my first or second wife, that I should have to marry so many times? Well, yes, there were, but they were very untrustworthy. Doris' son told me that Mariamne's two sons were plotting against me, so I had them disposed of. Several years later I found out that Doris' son had lied to me in order to cover up his own plot, so he had to be gotten rid of too. I tell you, I've been a victim of circumstances, more sinned against than sinning.

Then, when these wisemen came from the East speaking of another heir, you can bet I became interested. They spoke of a star they had seen in the East. My own thickheaded astrologers either had seen nothing or they had seen something and weren't telling me. I tried to imagine who else there was in the palace that I might have overlooked as a potential troublemaker. Then my advisors told me that there was a legend that one day a king would arise who had been born in Bethlehem. Well, I breathed easier; no one born in Bethlehem was going to make a difference in the world.

But then, I thought to myself, "You can't tell who people will listen to." So I called the Persian wisemen and told them they should go right away over to Bethlehem, a town about five miles away. I urged them, once they had found the one they were seeking, to come back here to Jerusalem to tell me where he was so that I might visit him as well. I thought that, if there was anything to what they said, it would be better to do what needed to be done quietly; you know, one night a soldier could slip into that house and dispose of the whole matter.

I know, the idea isn't a pleasant one. But it needed to be done for the good of the state! I mean, think what would happen if this nobody got wind of this legend and desired to become king. Could *he* be a realist? Would a simple peasant see the necessity of sacrificing for a cause, as I have sacrificed? Could he be expected to have convictions for which he would sacrifice his family? Would he be able to understand politics well enough to know that no one is to be trusted, that no one is a brother? The only safe rule is "Do others before they do you." Would he have known that? No, I dare say that he wouldn't. He might even have shared that quaint peasant notion that one ought to forgive one's enemies. Then there would be no respect for authority. For that reason, I never forgive. To rule well one must have connections, and one must be a realist.

A third qualification for a king is that he has to be firm. Take this incident over in Bethlehem. I asked those wisemen to come back and tell me where the child was. For some reason they didn't return. No doubt someone in my own palace led them to mistrust me. I waited several days. When they didn't return, I knew I had to act. I would have been satisfied simply to know where that one child was, but I couldn't very well go over to Bethlehem and ask the peasants. They have always been suspicious of me and will tell me nothing.

So I dispatched soldiers to Bethlehem to take care of the whole matter. I estimated that there would not be more than twenty male children in that town under two years of age. A small price to pay to preserve law and order in the realm. And so the act was done. I tell you, I did the world a favor.

What kind of king could he have become anyway? My advisors tell me that the Jewish Scriptures speak of a future Prince of Peace. What if *this* child had become *that*? He probably would go about teaching people to love their enemies. Really, where would that get us? All the world understands is power, force, and might. What would have happened to the state, or to my dynasty, if I had *loved* everybody? What would the Romans have done to me if all I spoke of was peace? Why, they probably would have crucified me, and I'd be forgotten. A king has to be firm when there is a threat, so I was firm about that child in Bethlehem.

    I know what you're thinking. There are some rumors that the child got away, but I doubt it. My soldiers are pretty thorough. But even if he did get away, he will never amount to much. As I said, a king must have important connections, be realistic about people, and be firm in action. I've got the important people on my side. Some people have said that God might support such a person. But you can take it from me, God isn't going to support an unknown peasant from Bethlehem!

    You've been questioning me about the death of that child and the others. Maybe you delight in finding me guilty there. But now I have a question for you. Suppose he does still live, this king from Bethlehem; whose way of life do you choose to follow, his, or mine?

Chapter Six

During the season of Advent the Lectionary provides numerous opportunities for a sermon about John the Baptist and his message. The heightened pageantry of the season makes a first person sermon especially appropriate. John is certainly a colorful character in his own right, and there are sufficient references to him in Scripture to provide us with a story line. But what might he have to say, beyond the telling of his own story, that would help members of a Christian congregation today to express their discipleship?

The differences in attitude, style, and message between Jesus and John provide a convenient outline for John to use as he gives his witness to who Jesus is. The fact that he did not fully understand the role of Jesus makes John a more authentic human being. John gives witness to as much of Jesus' ministry as he can understand. This leads him to make the point that we, too, are called to witness in the best way we can, even when we haven't got everything worked out to our satisfaction.

My objective in this sermon was to encourage people to share what they know of Christ. A one-sentence summary would be: "Contrasting the lives of John the Baptist and Jesus helps us to understand Jesus." Since much of the Scripture material about John comes from the later part of his ministry, I wanted to place this monologue as close to his death as possible without having him comment on his own death. I therefore imagined him in his prison cell, awaiting his end. To make the congregation aware of the fact that witness is sometimes given at great cost, I placed the following sentence in the worship folder under the sermon title: "John the Baptist was beheaded by King Herod prior to the crucifixion of Jesus for his outspoken criticism of the king's conduct."

John The Baptist

John 1:19-34

Sitting here in this cold, dark prison cell I have had a lot of time to think. When you're locked up, it makes you wonder if the direction your life has taken is the right one. I always thought that Jesus and I were on the same track, but as I sit here alone, I have come to see more clearly how we have differed. That has given me pause as I evaluate my life and ministry. I'd like to share some of those differences with you so that you can get a clearer picture of Jesus of Nazareth and the importance of his life for you.

The first thing that now occurs to me is how different our attitudes toward life have been. Some of that, I suppose, is a product of the things we were exposed to while growing up. My name is John Ben Zechariah. Some people call me John the Baptizer, or John the Baptist. John Ben Zechariah means John, son of Zechariah. My father was a priest who lived in the hill country of Judea, in southern Palestine. One day, when it was his turn to offer the sacrifice in the Temple at Jerusalem, he had a vision in which he was told that he was going to have a son, and that that son would have a special place in God's plan: that son would be a prophet. He was told to call the son John, and raise him as a Nazirite, which means someone who is dedicated to God, someone whose life is to be marked by purity. My mother's name was Elizabeth; she was a cousin of Mary, who later became the mother of Jesus. I was born about three months before Jesus was born.

Growing up as I did in the hill country of Judea, I often made my way to the desert area around the Dead Sea. There were situated there a number of small communities dedicated to purity of life. My contacts with these people became more and more frequent. As a result, these people had a significant impact on my view of the world. They taught me that life in the towns and cities was corrupt, so I learned to prefer the wilderness. They taught that good Jews must be scrupulous about keeping dietary laws, so I learned to eat the food of the desert — locust and wild honey —

and to avoid any compromise in diet. They taught that the soft life would make us ill-prepared to serve as God's soldiers, so I gave up soft clothing and took to wearing a camel skin. I became convinced that God wanted us Jews to avoid contact with Gentiles, to follow an austere lifestyle, to avoid anything that would corrupt us, and to focus on keeping the letter of God's law. Because of my zeal, I'm sure that a number of people who knew me thought of me as a crazy man.

Jesus, on the other hand, had a different set of experiences. He grew up in a town, and he accepted the fact that most people couldn't just pull up stakes and move out to the desert. He lived as ordinary people lived, he dressed as they did, ate what they ate, drank what they drank. In fact, his casual observance of the dietary laws made some people call him a glutton and a drunkard.

The town in which he grew up, Nazareth, is in the area called Galilee, a kind of commercial crossroads, subject to the customs of all kinds of people. In fact, we call the area "Galilee of the Gentiles." Because of these outside influences, it is a place where our kosher laws are often compromised. Jesus was known to eat without going through the ritual washing of hands we are supposed to observe. He was often at dinner parties and social gatherings. He associated with people that our more devout citizens called sinners. I felt that if a person took our religion very seriously, that person should avoid all those things. Jesus enjoyed life too much for a person who was supposed to be religious.

We also had different ways of dealing with people. When I was about 28 years old, I felt that God was calling me to preach to my people. I left the desert and began preaching along the Jordan River. I felt that people needed to be confronted with their sinfulness so that they would repent, but first I had to get their attention. Would you like to hear how I did that? I'd see a group of people and I would come up and challenge them: "You snakes! Who told you that you could escape from God's wrath that is about to come? Do the things that will show you have turned from your sins. And don't start saying among yourselves, 'Abraham is our ancestor,' as though that were all that is necessary to be on good terms with

God. I tell you that God can take these rocks and make descendants for Abraham!" That usually got their attention. I would point out ways in which they were breaking God's laws and I would tell them to repent because God's kingdom was at hand. People came out to the river by the hundreds to hear my message, to repent, and to ask what they could do to please God. I told them to be baptized — that is, to wash themselves in the Jordan River as a sign that they really wanted to be cleansed from their unrighteousness. Large numbers of people followed my advice.

Then, one day, Jesus showed up in the crowd and asked me to baptize *him*. This was before he embarked on his public ministry. I knew him, of course. He is my second cousin. His mother, Mary, and my mother, Elizabeth, were pregnant about the same time, and my family had told me that they expected something special from Jesus. But I hadn't seen him in quite a while. As soon as I saw him, something inside me said, "This is the one you have been proclaiming; this is the one who is going to deliver Israel." I was confused by this new thought. If he *were* the deliverer, *I* should be baptized by *him*. I suggested that, but he responded, "Let it be done this way for now." I consented, and as soon as he came up out of the water, there was some kind of mystical change about him, as though he had just resolved a great problem. The next thing he did was to go out and live in the desert for a while. I guess he was getting his thoughts together and planning his strategy.

About forty days later he returned to where I was preaching and I caught a glimpse of him in the crowd. I was anxious to see what he would do next. Israel needed a good house-cleaning, and if I had called people snakes to get their attention, he would no doubt be even more confrontational.

But that isn't the way he went about it. Instead of judging people, he affirmed them. Instead of convicting them of their sins, he seemed to accept people with all their weaknesses. Instead of emphasizing the law that was being broken, he stressed the love of God. Instead of keeping himself free from sinners, he included a hated tax collector and a terrorist among his close associates. He allowed a woman of doubtful reputation to have a place in his entourage. He said that

Zacchaeus, a known collaborator with the Romans, had a place in God's love. I did not understand his methods.

Our messages differed too. My message emphasized judgment. I told people that the ax was about to fall, that even the tree of Israel would be pruned to the very roots. "Every tree that does not bear good fruit," I said, "will be cut down and thrown into the fire." "Keeping God's law means everything," I would say, "and those who do not keep it will suffer God's wrath." I was out to reform sinners. How else could you do that if you didn't scare people into action?

Jesus, on the other hand, stressed the gracious acceptance of sinners by God. Instead of reforming sinners, he was out to redeem them. Instead of pouring judgment on people's failures, he spoke about the availability of an abundant life. He seemed to be wooing people into the Kingdom rather than scaring them into it. He preferred the carrot to the stick, but I didn't have much confidence that his message would change people. If he *were* the Messiah, he ought to be taking some significant action.

Not long after Jesus began his public ministry, I was arrested because I criticized Herod, the ruler of our province, for taking his brother's wife. I have been sitting here in this prison cell, day after day, waiting for word that Jesus was getting on with the business of being the Messiah. If he *is* God's special person, you would think he would begin to take action against everything that is contrary to God's will. You'd expect some evidence of God's power.

Some of my closest followers are allowed to come and visit me in this prison cell. They tell me what is going on out in the world. One day recently I became so discouraged at Jesus' inaction that I sent some of my followers to Jesus with a question: "Are you who we think you are or not? Are you going to show yourself or should we look for somebody else?"

Jesus was not about to be pressured to do what *we* wanted him to do. Instead, he spoke unapologetically to my friends and said, "Go and tell John what you hear and see: the blind receive their sight, the lame walk, lepers are cleansed, the deaf hear, the dead are raised up and the poor have good news preached to them."

It has become apparent to me that Jesus is not going to do things my way. Our style, our methods, our message differ from each other. Is he right? Was I wrong? These are thoughts that have been running through my mind since my friends returned with Jesus' response.

Fortunately, God has helped me to resolve my doubts about Jesus and about my own calling. Sitting here, my mind took me back to an incident that happened shortly after I baptized Jesus. Some authorities from the Temple in Jerusalem came out to question me at the Jordan River. They wanted to check out the correctness of my beliefs, and also to find out what kind of aspirations I might have, if any. All kinds of strange stories had built up about who I was and what I was doing. By then I had a number of loyal followers, and I suppose the authorities were afraid I might lead some sort of revolt.

So they came right out and asked me, "Are you the Messiah?" I answered, "I am not the Messiah."

"Are you Elijah, then?" they asked, for our Scriptures state that Elijah will return ahead of the Messiah. I answered that I was not Elijah either, though I know that Jesus did later refer to me as one who came in the spirit and power of Elijah.

"Are you that other prophet?" they asked, referring to a statement made by Moses that one day a prophet would arise who would be like Moses. "No," I said, "I am not that prophet either."

"Well, then, who are you?" they insisted. For the first time my role suddenly became clear to me. I was not destined to be the leader of some great movement; I was to serve as a proclaimer of someone else. So I answered them with words from the prophet Isaiah. I said, "I am the voice of one who shouts in the desert: 'Make straight a path for the Lord to travel.'" I was to be a herald, one who goes out ahead of a king to make the province ready for his coming.

It's strange. I hadn't thought about that incident until my friends returned with Jesus' response. Now the recollection of it gives me much comfort. My own words remind me of my role. I am not the savior of the world. I am simply a voice called to give testimony to what God is doing in the world. I had to do what I did my way because of who I am. If my methods were imperfect, I am sorry for that. All I have wanted to do is to catch people's attention.

I do not know if I will ever get out of this cell. If I do not, that will be all right. I have done what I was called to do. I have been a voice calling people to prepare, to make a place for God in their lives. I may not always have fully understood what God was intending to do, but I have been faithful to the best of my understanding.

I have also been a pointer, not pointing to myself, but to the one whose way I was preparing. One day, when I was preaching by the Jordan River, I saw Jesus in the crowd. I pointed to him and said, "There is the lamb of God." Immediately, two of my followers left me and followed Jesus. That was a hard thing for me to accept, but it has become clear to me that that is as it should be. *He* must increase, and *I* must decrease.

There is a lesson here for all who have come to appreciate Jesus. We are to be voices, witnesses to those around us. We are to be pointers to the one who is making a difference in our lives. *I* did it in *my* way; *you* do it in *yours*. But however it occurs to you to do it, *do* it.

Chapter Seven

Judas has long been an enigma. What could cause a person, who had been so close to Jesus, willingly to betray him into the hands of his enemies? Trying to get inside the mind of Judas may help us to understand him and to understand some things about ourselves. Judas may have had a certain expectation of who Jesus was and how he should conduct himself. When Jesus did not fulfill those expectations, Judas may have felt that he could set up a situation in which Jesus would have to act in order to save himself and advance his kingdom. At the same time, Jesus would be advancing Judas' agenda. Have we not, from time to time, wanted to manipulate God in a way that would advance our own agenda? There is something of Judas in each of us.

I chose to have Judas tell his story from a point close to his own death, but before he had decided what he would do. This would allow him maximum time to contemplate what he had done and to draw a lesson for others from his own experience. Beyond telling us his story, Judas is able to caution us about our own ambition and our assumption that we can make God do what we want God to do. A one-sentence summary of what I was attempting to accomplish in the sermon would be: "Judas had expected great things from his association with Jesus, but when they did not materialize, he attempted to force Jesus' hand, only to become involved in Jesus' death."

The Betrayer

Mark 14:1-4; Matthew 27:1-10

I always felt that I was the outsider. I was the Southerner. All the others, including Jesus, were from Galilee in the north. I alone was different, and they never let me forget it! My name is Judas, son of Simon, but they always called me Iscariot, meaning "the man from the village of Kerioth" in the south. I alone was a Judean. I was, until recently, a follower of Jesus of Nazareth. Many of us thought that he would bring in the new order and rule Israel.

Now everything has changed, for I betrayed the very one I had been following and brought an end to the dream! I didn't really mean to betray him. Things went farther than I intended. I have discovered that it is easier than you may think to betray your master. But that gets ahead of my story. Please, I have to talk to someone. Listen to me for a while. What I have to say may help you to avoid the tragedy into which I fell.

I had come to expect great things from this Jesus. He was a young man on the way up. At first I watched him from the edge of the crowd. I was there when he stood up in the synagogue in his home town and announced that he was the fulfillment of the Jewish Scriptures. I saw the determination in his face and I heard the authority in his voice. The townspeople thought it was blasphemy, and they took him out to a cliff to throw him over, but he got away from them. I marked that well — his ability to escape.

I was in the crowd when he gave that great sermon on the mount. You remember how he spoke of the blessed life: blessed are the poor, the meek, the hungry, the thirsty, the persecuted. That was enough to set afire the zeal of any young man: blessed are the down and outers. That was for me. He wanted to correct the inequities and abuses in life — and so did I.

One day he called for volunteers to go out and preach the good news of God's love, and I enthusiastically responded. There were seventy of us in all; we went out two by two. Our success was phenomenal! People listened, and their lives were changed. We prayed for the demon-possessed and their minds were straightened out. We prayed for the sick and they improved. What power we had! We returned and told Jesus of our good success. He said, "I know. I saw Satan falling through your work." I was delirious with the power that had been given to us. I decided then and there to attach myself to him permanently. I followed him everywhere.

Then, one day, he began to call some of his followers aside by name. He wanted an inner circle to travel with him full-time. Obviously, he was developing a cadre of informed insiders. He called eleven of the seventy. They were men I knew: Peter, James, John, Andrew. One by one I watched them go to him. Then, lastly, he called me, Judas of Kerioth. Not only did he wish me to be his disciple, he wanted me, with my business experience, to be treasurer of the group. If anyone made contributions to our work, I was to carry the money. If any purchases were to be made, I would make them. What a stepping stone that would be! When the revolution came and he was swept to power, I might be treasurer of all Israel. He was a revolutionary, you know. He talked constantly about the Kingdom of Heaven that was to come; and he was to be in the middle of it. He saw signs of the coming Kingdom in everything: in yeast expanding in dough; in a seed growing silently in the ground; in a harvest where the weeds are separated from the good stalks. I was sure that his declaration of his reign was just around the corner.

One day out by the Sea of Galilee, he fed 5,000 people from very little food. I could see his design in it: an army marches on its stomach, and he was experimenting to see if he could meet the demand. The people went wild. Some wanted to make him king right there, but he put them off. I guess he felt that the time wasn't right. I was disappointed, but I felt that he knew best.

Another time we were at Caesarea Philippi. He took Peter, James, and John with him to a hill, where his appearance was changed into something different before their very eyes. I didn't see it, but the others said that Elijah, the prophet, and Moses, the Lawgiver, were there, and that God himself spoke to them. I knew what it meant. It meant that he was going to present himself as a prophet and lawgiver, and he would have God himself on his side.

Any moment, I thought, he would declare himself. Only he didn't. He simply decided to go to Jerusalem. That was not new; we had been there three times before in his short public life. Surely this time his star would rise.

But instead, things began to go badly. Some people began to circulate the rumor that Jesus was really John the Baptist. Of course that was ridiculous. John had been beheaded by Herod. But Herod had a guilty conscience. He wanted to see Jesus personally in order to satisfy his conscience, so he placed patrols on the main highway to Jerusalem in order to seize Jesus, if possible. We had to go out of our way to avoid them.

Moreover, Jesus had offended the religious authorities, and they, too, were out to get him. Not that I was afraid, you understand. After all, God was on his side. I was all for his taking over right there. Why go to all the trouble of going to Jerusalem? But no, he wouldn't do that. So we turned aside for a while into Samaria, a disgusting place. The people there received us very well, until they learned we were on our way to Jerusalem. You see, they have their own temple on Mount Gerizim, and they figured if that wasn't good enough for Jesus, he could leave. So we were forced out of Samaria. If I had been Jesus, I would have called down fire on them, even as James and John suggested.

We couldn't follow the main road because of Herod's soldiers, so we crossed the Jordan River and continued south on the other side. Here we were, in the company of a potential king, and we were forced out of our own land! I was losing patience with Jesus.

We crossed the Jordan again at Jericho and re-entered our holy land just as Joshua had done so many centuries before, when he came as a conquering hero. You know, Jesus's own name could be pronounced Joshua, or Jehoshua. It means "God saves." For me, this crossing was highly symbolic. I saw Jesus fulfilling the role of an earlier conqueror.

We eventually came to the home of some of his friends in Bethany. While we were there, one of his friends, Mary, came and poured a vase full of expensive perfume on Jesus as he reclined at the table. I protested the waste involved. If she *really* wanted to advance our work, she should have given *me* the perfume, and I would have sold it and used the money to meet our needs. What if things didn't go as we expected in Jerusalem? We would need all we could get to tide us over. But Jesus defended her. He said that this was preparation for his death. I didn't understand that talk, and I certainly didn't like it.

The next day we left for Jerusalem. Finally, things were beginning to look up. Jesus borrowed a donkey so that he could enter Jerusalem with some dignity. And, just as I expected, the crowds poured out of the city to greet him. Some of us put our robes down on the roadway in front of him. Other people cut down palm branches, symbols associated with the rulers of Israel, and waved them in the air as Jesus approached the city gates. All of us were uttering cries of joyous acclamation, "Hosanna," which means "O save!" At last Jesus was coming into his own — and we with him, of course.

But I think he lost his nerve. There was the crowd — a perfect time to declare himself. We all would have testified to his greatness. But he let the moment pass. All he did was go and drive a few dishonest merchants out of the Temple. He really let me down: Judas Iscariot, Treasurer of all Israel, was likely to wind up a nothing, all because Jesus lost his nerve.

It was then that I became involved in a plot. I knew the priests were after him. And I knew they couldn't take him in the daytime; he was too popular for that. So I went to them with a deal: I would tell them where to find him at night, away from the crowds. Don't ask me why I did it; I don't know why anymore. It wasn't the money; that was just to seal the bargain. I guess I was disappointed because he refused to be king. And as long as *he* refused, *I* was nothing. So I sought to force his hand, back him to the wall; then he would call on God, Moses, Elijah, and everyone else to come to his aid. I was convinced that he needed me to get the action started.

For several nights our pattern had been the same. We would leave the city for Bethany, two miles away, stopping over in the Garden of Gethsemane on the way. It was now Thursday. The next day was a special feast. I knew the time had come to act. The authorities would not want to act on the following evening, Friday, because the Sabbath would have begun. Thursday had to be the time.

That evening at dinner, Jesus knew something was up. He said, "One of you will betray me." Then he said to me, "What you are going to do, do quickly." He knew! I couldn't stand to stay in his presence. I needed some fresh air, so I left, pretending that I had a special errand to run. One day he would understand. He would thank me for forcing him to act.

I ran to the priests and told them that they would be able to find Jesus later that evening in Gethsemane. That was all I was supposed to do. I wanted to get back to our small company so that the other disciples wouldn't give much thought to my absence. But now information was not enough. The priests didn't want to be personally involved in going after Jesus. They were afraid there might be trouble. Instead, they had decided to send the temple guards. But the guards didn't know Jesus. They would need someone who could identify him for them. I was in too deep now to back out. I consented to identify Jesus with a kiss. When he used his power, as he surely would, he would recognize that my motive was to get him to act.

When we came to the Garden, Jesus and the other disciples were already there. I walked up and said, "Hail, Master," and I kissed him. He said, "Friend, why are you here?" Think of it. He knew what I was doing, and he called me "friend." But there wasn't time to explain. The soldiers advanced; Peter attempted to defend him, but Jesus forbade him, and the disciples ran off in fright. I alone stood by to see him use his power. But none was used. He went away peaceably, and I was left to ponder my fate.

I wandered most of the night, asking myself: "What does a betrayer do?" Toward morning I came across some servants from the Temple. They were fashioning a cross. It was for Jesus, they said, whom they were sure Pilate would condemn to death. It then came to me what I had done! By my actions I had placed Jesus in the hands of his enemies. Of course he would not destroy them; he had taught us to love our enemies, for this was God's way. It was clear now that he would sacrifice his own life rather than deprive them of theirs.

I ran to the Temple and threw down the money, but the priests would not take it back. I cried, "I have sinned by betraying innocent blood." "That's your affair," they said, and left me to myself.

Jesus they took out and crucified. That is why I stand before you this morning. I am afraid to be alone, afraid of what I might do or think. I do not know what will become of me.

At least let me do this much. Let me warn you to take thought of your lives. Every one of us is capable of betraying our master, of killing the very thing we love. We do that when we refuse to accept Jesus as he is and try to make him into what we want him to be. We do that when we insist on doing by force what can only be accomplished by love. We do that when we allow our personal ambition to take precedence over our call to be of service.

None of us deliberately plots to hurt the one we follow, but when our instincts, our selfishness, our pride get out of hand, we can say and do cruel things that betray him. Take heed, then, to yourselves, so that in your moment of opportunity you may be more faithful than I.

Chapter Eight

Bible dictionaries and commentaries are able to give us a little extra-biblical information about Pontius Pilate, so that we may augment the biblical materials with some elements of his life before he arrived in Palestine and after he departed. Added to that is the legend that he retired to a villa on Lake Lucerne, where a mountain bears his name. Whether he ever thought of Jesus after the trial we do not know, but if he was in fact forced to depart Rome and live in exile, he may have thought back on many of his mistakes and missed opportunities, the trial of Jesus among them.

For purposes of this sermon I imagined Pilate as an older, subdued servant of an empire that no longer welcomed him. He is disillusioned with politics and power. Certainly, he has had much opportunity for reflection. He does more than simply tell us his story; he gives testimony to the importance of integrity. The one-sentence summary that guided the development of this sermon is: "In spite of pressures to decide against Jesus, Pilate's sad story shows the importance of deciding for him."

Because some of the material in the sermon was based on legend, I included the following statement in the worship folder under the sermon title: "Legend says that Pontius Pilate died in exile near Lake Lucerne, and that on certain moonlit nights his body rises to the surface of the lake, endlessly washing hands that will not become clean."

Pilate's Story

Matthew 27:15-24

How good of you to come and see me. I'm surprised that anyone remembers us now. "Pontius Pilate and his wife Claudia," that is the way they used to announce us in Rome. But, since retirement, we don't get there much anymore. And what with Claudia's condition and all, it is better to stay here around Lake Lucerne. The Alpine air is just what the doctor ordered. Well, maybe not *just* what the doctor ordered. To tell the truth, it's what Caesar ordered. And it isn't so much retirement either; it's exile. We would love to be in Rome, but we can't go there. We are out of favor, and we are obliged to stay here. You see, there were some things that happened while I was serving in my last post — in Judea. Let me tell you about them.

I had thought I was doing rather well — a soldier rising from the middle class. I married Claudia, a granddaughter of Tiberius Caesar. She was a true aristocrat. I remember her own grandfather telling me at the wedding: "The best move a politician can make is to marry well." Eventually, I was appointed procurator of Judea, not a major assignment, but certainly a stepping-stone. I was anxious to do well — to represent Rome with strength, efficiency, peace, and justice. I hoped during my tenure to gain enough in taxes and other benefits to live well upon our return to Rome.

From the beginning, it didn't go well. The ones who ran the country were the priests. As soon as I arrived in Caesarea, the administrative capital, a delegation came to see me. The high priest, Caiaphas, even loaned me money, "to meet my many expenses," he said. I soon learned that he had hooked me and would endlessly expect favors. I soon learned to bluff, scheme, cheat, and hate.

Soon after my arrival, I went up to Jerusalem. I discovered that, because of their religious peculiarities, there were no images of Caesar in the city. It was the only major city in the entire empire where that was so. I felt that was a situation which needed to be corrected, so one night I had some of my soldiers place large portraits of the emperor on the towers of the fortress, overlooking the

Temple. The next day, 6,000 Jews gathered outside the fortress, praying and chanting for the removal of the portraits. It went on day and night. For five days, I refused to see them. Then, I told them to disperse, or I would have them killed. All 6,000 of them bared their necks and dared me to do it. I couldn't have word get back to Rome that I had killed 6,000 unarmed civilians, so I took down the portraits. But when word got back to Rome, *I* was perceived to have caused the problem. From that time on, I dreaded feast days, for every one brought new threats of revolt.

To get on the good side of the Jews, I suggested building an aqueduct to bring water to Jerusalem. The priests readily agreed. Since it was for their benefit, I took the funds from their temple treasury. Again, the Jews raised a protest. They were good at that. To keep it from becoming a riot, I sent soldiers, dressed as peasants, into the crowd with clubs. They beat the ringleaders and, without leaders, the protest lost momentum. Unfortunately, some Jews were hurt, and a few died. When word got back to Rome, the emperor was outraged and rebuked me for poor judgment. I learned to hate those priests, and I tried to thwart them at every turn.

During their Passover several years ago, Claudia and I went up to Jerusalem for the feast. One night Caiaphas came to me to talk about a case he was interested in. There was a man from Nazareth, named Jesus, whom the priests had been watching. They said that he was some kind of pretender to the Jewish throne. They had already arrested him, and tried him that night. He was found guilty of blasphemy, a charge I didn't understand. I told them to take care of it themselves; they had the power. But they didn't want to be the ones to kill him. They said he was seditious — a political threat. They wanted me to hear the case and to find him guilty. Some justice, right? They wanted me to try him, and they were already telling me the verdict. I told him I wouldn't be part of their scheme. It was then that he reminded me of the loan. Moreover, he said, either I would convict the prisoner, or there would be a riot. The proud arm of Roman justice was to be a dirty dagger in the hands of those scheming priests.

When he left, Claudia and I talked. She said she knew of the man whom the priests wanted dead. The slave girl, who fixed her hair, had told her about him. A harmless fellow, a traveling preacher. Claudia has always been interested in talk of gods and such. She said she was quite taken by some of the interesting things she had heard about him. We didn't sleep much that night. We talked of Rome and parties, of career and compromise, and of the villa we hoped one day to own.

The next morning Caiaphas and his cronies came to the hall that I used when I judged cases in Jerusalem. They had several guards and a prisoner with his hands tied. The prisoner had obviously already been through interrogation. "What's the charge?" I said. "What difference does it make?" muttered Caiaphas. "We wouldn't have brought him to you if he weren't guilty." "Then judge him yourself," I said. I thought there should be some semblance of justice. The priest rolled his eyes toward the prisoner and whispered, "Don't you remember what we talked about last night? Do I need to go through all that again?"

"Are you the King of the Jews?" I asked the prisoner. "So you say," he responded. "It must be so," I said. "Your own people have handed you over to me." "My kingship is not of this world," he responded. "If it were, my servants would fight." Sensing that no case was being made, the priests began to list the charges: perverting the nation; forbidding the payment of tribute to Caesar; saying that he was Christ, a king. "So, you are a king then?" I said. "I am a witness to the truth," he answered. That phrase caught me. I had been looking for the truth all my life. For a while, I thought I knew what it was, but now it eluded me and left an emptiness. I had been in Judea for six years, and this was the first time I had found anyone interested in the truth. "What is truth?" I asked the prisoner. He didn't answer me. He just looked at me as though he doubted I would understand, even if he told me.

"Don't you hear the things they are saying about you?" I said. "Don't you want to make a defense?" He only looked at me. He answered nothing. I looked him over carefully. "I don't find any crime in him," I said. Caiaphas was enraged. "This is not going as we discussed it," he whispered. "He stirs up the people from Jerusalem to Galilee." "Is he from Galilee?" I asked. "Well, that's the territory of Herod, and he is down here for the holidays. Let's have *him* hear the case."

I sent the whole group off to Herod. The priests were livid that things hadn't gone as they planned, but there was nothing they could do about it.

While they were away, my wife sent me a message. After our late-night conversation, she had had bad dreams about the case and was urging me to beg off. "Don't do anything rash," she advised. "We've already had enough trouble here." I looked out the window from the judgment hall and noticed that quite a crowd was gathering in the courtyard below. Were they likely to be friends of this Nazarene, I wondered, or enemies?

Before long, the entourage returned from Herod, dissatisfied. He had been interested in interviewing the Nazarene, because the fellow was from his region. But Herod wasn't about to touch the case. "I'll be interested to see what you decide," he said. The prisoner was wearing a crown made out of thorn branches. Some of the thorns had pierced his skin, and there were small streams of blood on his brow. They had thrown an old cape over his shoulders. Even under those circumstances, there was something regal about the way he bore up under all this. For a moment, I wanted to spring to my feet and salute him. It occurred to me that the priests might settle for a compromise. "Herod has found nothing in the charges deserving of death," I said, "and neither do I. Why don't I have my soldiers rough him up a bit, teach him a lesson, show him we don't want any foolishness, and then let him go?" But that was not what they had in mind. This traveling preacher had challenged their authority, and they wanted him dead.

Still, I was not prepared to give in to them. It was my custom to show clemency on this feast day by releasing a prisoner in recognition of the Jewish release from captivity in Egypt. We had a fellow in custody by the name of Barabbas, an insurrectionist and murderer. "I am supposed to release a prisoner today," I announced. "It was going to be Barabbas. Why don't we make it Jesus instead?" But those crafty priests insisted that it be Barabbas.

"Why don't we see what the people say to that?" I suggested. I took Jesus out onto the balcony overlooking the courtyard below.

Signaling for the attention of the crowd, I called out: "Look at this man. He's called 'The King of the Jews.' Today I am going to release a prisoner. Should it be the King of the Jews or Barabbas?" At first the crowd wasn't sure what to say, but some of the priests, who had come out onto the balcony, began to shout, "Barabbas." Before long, the crowd had joined in the chant: "Barabbas." "And what shall I do with the King of the Jews?" I asked. "Crucify him!" shouted the priests. And soon the whole crowd was shouting, "Crucify him!"

I never could understand those people. I stepped back into the judgment hall. "By all rights this man should be set free," I said to the priests. "We have a law," said Caiaphas, "and by our law he ought to die, because he made himself out to be the Son of God." I looked over at the prisoner, now visibly weakened by his several beatings. He didn't look like a Son of God. "Where are you from anyway?" I asked him. He didn't answer me. "Don't you know that I have the power to release you or to crucify you?" I asked. "Your power over me comes from above," he said. What did *that* mean, I wondered: that my power came from the emperor? Of course, that was true. Or did he mean that my power came from the gods? Or as those Jews would have it, from their *one* God, who they felt ruled over everything? Well, for me, Caesar was both ruler and god. And it was in *his* name that I governed.

"I believe I'll release him," I said. "If you release him, you're no friend of Caesar," responded Caiaphas. "He has made himself out to be a king, and that puts him against the Emperor." It was pretty clear what he was saying. Whatever I decided that day was going to be reported to Rome, and it had better sound like I was supporting the Emperor's interests. "Do you want me to crucify your king?" I asked. "We have no king but Caesar," Caiaphas responded with an obsequious smile. What a laugh! This stiff-necked people, always on the verge of revolt, were so determined to get rid of that helpless prophet that they were willing to profess loyalty to the Emperor.

I was in a tough spot. Down in the courtyard, the crowd was becoming agitated. A riot could easily have broken out. Roman law would have supported releasing the man, but those priests could make it appear that I was not attentive to the Emperor's interest. My wife, with her religious sensibilities, had urged caution. The man was basically a decent fellow who had gotten crossways with the priests.

My career was on the line. If I did what I felt would be the right thing to do and let him go, I could lose my position. I needed some kind of dramatic action that could get me off the hook. I took a pitcher of water and a basin out onto the balcony, poured water into the basin, washed my hands in front of the crowd and said, "I am innocent of this man's blood. Do with him what you will." Oh, if only it could be that easy to absolve oneself of responsibility! I have discovered that to go against conscience leaves a stain that is not so easily washed away.

I stepped back inside, signed the order releasing Barabbas, and signed the order for the execution of the King of the Jews. The priests had won. As the party was about to lead the prisoner away, I told them to wait a moment. I took a piece of papyrus and wrote the words "King of the Jews" on it. "Put this at the top of the cross," I said. "It will identify his crime." Caiaphas, who was momentarily satisfied with the way things were working out, took exception to the statement. "Why don't you write, 'He said I am King of the Jews'?" I hadn't won much that day. If the statement dissatisfied the priests, so much the better. "Let it be as I have written it," I said.

As they left, the Nazarene looked at me. He said nothing, but the look in his eyes was one of pity rather than hatred. He glanced at my hands. I'll feel the weight of his eyes on my hands for as long as I live. He knew, and I knew, that justice had not been served that day. Both of us were victims. I should have judged in his favor, but I felt that I couldn't afford to. As a result, justice and truth both suffered.

I never saw the Nazarene again, although I've seen him often in my thoughts. And Claudia — she has seen him often in her dreams. Poor Claudia. She was overwhelmed by the whole thing. She feels that I condemned some kind of spiritual king. Since that time, Claudia has become afraid of the dark. She can sleep only in a lighted room. You see, the day the Nazarene was executed, the daylight vanished! The sun just went away for several hours. I don't know how or why. I only know that it became dark as a cave as I was trying to explain to Claudia why I had to do what I did. But she only railed at me about her dream. Since then, we have felt as though we were under a curse.

I wasn't much good at governing after that. A short time after the execution of that country preacher, there was a disturbance in Samaria. I felt that the Samaritans were about to revolt, so I sent soldiers to break up a gathering at their temple. They resisted; there was violence; some of them were killed and fell on the altar where they were making a sacrifice. "Sacrificed on their own altar." That's how the word got back to Rome.

The emperor felt that I had had more than enough opportunity to make things work in Judea. I was called home, and then sent here to Lucerne, far from Rome, to live out my exile. It isn't so bad, really. Oh, we miss Rome, but the air here is good. It is supposed to cure whatever ails you. One problem is that there is so much time here to think. I walk by the lake. I put my hands in the water and I am reminded again of that day in Jerusalem. Nothing will wash it away.

I have relived that day a thousand times. If I had it to do over again, it would be different. Does that surprise you? Pilate, the hard-bitten Roman soldier, the proud, career-oriented politician, has feelings of remorse? Well, it's true! Power, wealth, prestige, physical well-being, all those things with which we Romans are so occupied — they are all fleeting. I was anxious to have all of them, so I forfeited other things: honor, justice, truth, personal integrity, for material advancement, and I lost it all. That Nazarene spoke of a kingdom not of this world, a realm where justice and truth and integrity are valued, but I was too busy trying to keep my position to pay much attention to what he had to say. Yes, sir, if I could do it over, I'd sit at his feet and listen to what *he* had to say.

You know, sometimes I have the feeling that he is near, that one day I'll turn around and he will be there, and I'll tell him I handled things badly, and he'll listen and understand. Maybe that kingdom he spoke about is not so far away. I missed it once. I won't miss it again.

Chapter Nine

Many people are acquainted with the fact that there was once a gentle soul by the name of Francis of Assisi who loved birds and animals, but they may have little awareness of where he lived, when he lived, or what he did. Such ignorance does not serve us well. In a day when heroes are determined by their capacity for violence or self-indulgence, we need to know that there have been people who have attempted to conduct themselves according to the teachings of Christ and that those people have made a difference in the world.

Reading several books on Francis gave me more than enough material. It was then necessary to ask what he might have to say to people today. His simple faith, humility, gentleness, and appreciation for nature make him appealing to this generation. My working proposition became: "Francis of Assisi shows us how to respond to the challenges of self-conquest, meaningful work, setting priorities, sharing our faith, and finding God." In order that the congregation might experience the spirituality of Francis, I included "A Thanksgiving Of Saint Francis," "The Prayer Of Saint Francis," and his hymn "All Creatures Of Our God And King" among the worship elements used that day. I felt that the two Scripture passages were illuminated by his life. So that people would know that service to God is very demanding, I included the following sentence under the sermon title in the worship folder: "Francis of Assisi died in 1226 at the age of 44."

Francis Of Assisi

Psalm 24:1-6; Matthew 10:5-14

One day, in the year 1205, a well-dressed young man of 23 guided his horse out of the city of Assisi and into the plain below. He was heading for the Lazaretto, the place where lepers were required to live. The young man trembled as he rode, as though he were proceeding to meet his destiny. He had traveled this way many times before to give small gifts of money to the poor unfortunates who lived in such desperate circumstances, but these gifts had really been payments to his own conscience. This day was to be different. As a leper approached, holding out his emaciated arms for alms, the young man, mustering up all his courage, leaped from his horse, embraced the leper, and kissed him. Only if you feel some of the horror which leprosy aroused in that vain, exhibitionist, snobbish young man can you measure the magnitude of this single act of self-conquest. It was a major turning point in that young man's life. Learning to love what he loathed, he was enabled thereafter to set aside his own personal desires. In conquering himself, he had conquered the world.

I know these things to be true, for I am that young man. I was baptized Giovanni Bernardone, but from the very beginning I was nicknamed Francesco, "The Frenchman," because my mother was French. Most people call me simply Francis of Assisi. From the very beginning of my life my parents indulged me. My father was a well-to-do cloth merchant, who expected that one day I would take over his business. I was always well-dressed, because that advertised my father's business. I always had plenty of money to spend, always out looking for a good time, a playboy, a leader in revelries.

My dream was to be a knight. That was unlikely, for though we were well-off, we were not nobles, and it was rare for a commoner to be a knight. Nevertheless, in 1202, at the age of twenty, I thought my opportunity had come. Assisi went to war with the nearby town, Perugia. I entered the battle, hoping for glory. Instead,

I was captured by the enemy. I spent a year in a filthy prison cell. I kept jovial for a while, but eventually my health broke in those dreadful circumstances and I was released to return home. I regained my physical strength, but I lost my former zest for living. Things that formerly had given me delight lost their old magic. Things were going well at home, but I was in a terrible depression.

A year later I joined another military expedition, this time going to Sicily. I got as far as Spoleto, thirty miles away, when an overwhelming sense of the futility of all this came upon me. I had a dream which convinced me that I should return to Assisi and find my future there. I returned, and shortly after, I attended a feast, but I was no longer a riotous companion. Increasingly, the realization was coming on me that life was meant to be something other than having a good time.

It was just such thoughts about having one's life account for something which led to the incident with the leper. It is not a course of action I prescribe for anyone else, but it was my way of responding to a challenge that we must all face in the difficult task of self-conquest, the call to move from irresponsibility to responsibility, from self-centeredness to other-centeredness. For me, it was not simply a single act, it was the beginning of a new day of life, for from that time on I did all I could to minister to lepers, a group of people I learned to love. Increasingly, I sought places of solitary prayer and meditation, and these I found in abundance in the old, half-abandoned chapels around Assisi.

It was in one of those old chapels that I received my second challenge. I prayed often in the tumbled-down church of San Damiano. One day as I prayed, I felt sure I saw the lips of the crucifix move. I heard our Lord saying, "Francis, you see that my house is falling down. Go and repair it for me." I answered, "Willingly, Lord." I ran back to my father's store, took as many bolts of material as I could carry, and ran off to sell them at a reduced price in a neighboring town to get money for supplies. I even sold my horse and had to walk back to Assisi.

In my zeal, I lost all my senses. I was so excited at the prospect of doing something worthwhile that I did not stop to think of how my father would feel. My father was furious. He felt that he had been robbed and came to the little church where I was staying to get me and have me put in jail. I fled from my father and lived in a cave for a month, where I had a lot of time to think.

When I finally came back to town, most of my friends felt I had gone mad. My father put me in a cell in our house until I should come to trial, but my mother helped me escape and I returned to San Damiano, asking the priest to receive me into the religious life.

It was the bishop who finally called me to trial. He required me to return the money to my father, which I did. It was apparent to me that I could no longer live under my father's supervision; he had one set of expectations for me, I had another. Now was the time to act in a dramatic and public way so that I would not be tempted to give up on my newly chosen path, so I publicly took off all my clothes, piled them neatly, returned them to my father with thanks, and stood naked before the bishop. "Now at last," I said, "I can look to our Father in heaven to provide and no longer to my father, Pietro di Bernardone." The bishop put his cloak around me and accepted me into the religious life.

Thereafter, I spent much time in prayer and meditation, seeking to find my destiny. I wore old and tattered clothing as a part of my rejection of my past style of life. A friend gave me a coarse, brown tunic, a pair of sandals, a leather belt and a walking stick; from that point on, that is what I wore.

I returned to the church of San Damiano in Assisi to carry out what the crucifix had told me to do. I begged for building materials from the people of Assisi and received them. I was frightened, I was mocked by my own family, but the people responded, many joining me in the hard work of restoring the church. When that was done, I repaired another church, and then another, taking several years. But all during this time something was happening. I felt I was doing what I should be doing, that it was worthwhile. But I began to see that there was a far greater task than putting stone on stone in disused churches. The real church was people, ordinary men and women bound together in the mystical body of Christ, whose hearts were in need of rebuilding.

I tell you these things, not to get you to do things the way I did, but to demonstrate that every one of us is challenged to do something worthwhile. I took my challenge quite literally at first and repaired churches. You too, I am sure, are called to do something worthwhile. I was wrong to try to make my father pay for what I wanted to do; each of us must find our own place and fill it, not expect others who do not share our vision to participate. But there is something for every one of us to do.

My third challenge came after I had repaired a 700-year-old Benedictine chapel that we called "the little portion." While participating in the mass one day, I heard the priest read that part of the Gospel of Matthew in which Jesus urges his followers to go and preach and to take no staff, no sandals, no extra tunic. "This is what I have been waiting for," I thought. I took off my shoes, threw away my staff, replaced my leather belt with a piece of rope, and set out to preach the gospel. I sought no followers, yet there were those who desired to be my companions. We set up simple rules based on the Bible. "Sell what you have and give to the poor. Go and preach, taking nothing for your journey. Take up your cross and follow Christ." It was the only way we knew to divorce ourselves from the temptations of the flesh and of money. Within a year there were twelve of us, eleven laymen and one priest. Always, our order would be essentially one of laymen. We set out to preach, two by two, calling ourselves the "Penitents of Assisi." We were in love with God and all God's handiwork: the world, nature, animals, and people! We urged all to love and fear the Creator and to keep God's commandments.

In time, women also came seeking admission to our order. First among them was Clare Scipioni, who started a convent for religious women at the San Damiano church. Their order came to be known as the "Poor Clares." The order for men, which we called the "fratres minores" or "lesser brethren," were permitted to use "the little portion," which I mentioned earlier, as our headquarters. A third order was established for people who agreed with our basic views of simple life, but who did not wish to enter the cloistered life.

I don't want you to think that I expect everyone to enter the religious life, but I do think that every Christian is called upon to share the gospel of love in some way. Some will do it by preaching, others by deeds of mercy and compassion. I do not think that every Christian should take the vow of poverty, but I do think that every Christian is being challenged to set priorities in his or her life. What comes first, God or money? What do you love more, things or people? What does your style of life say about what you believe?

Another challenge I had to face was the challenge of organized religion. I had not sought to develop an order. Yet, as I have said, many chose to be a part of my work. We tried to keep things simple. Certain verses of Scripture were our guide. Members of our order left our house and went all over the world proclaiming the love of God. The church began to insist that our requirements were too harsh, that we needed a written rule or standard, something that could be interpreted, and that we needed to have an organization with someone in charge. I did not want the responsibility, but I was placed in charge and told to write a rule for our order. I put it off as long as I could. What I had was a simple and personal revelation; if others wanted to join me, well and good; if they thought the expectations were too stern, let them not participate, but why should a spirit of freedom be stifled by rules? Alas, it was to no avail. I resisted the necessity of a written rule for as long as I could, but the more people we had working with us, the more insistent the church was that we should have a rule, so finally, one was adopted.

I tell you this because it is the common lot of every good idea. One person can do something in an unorganized manner if he wishes, but when others come to join that person, inevitably organization is required. The person who first had the idea will spend less and less time doing what he feels called to do, and more and more time giving direction. I wanted to go out as a missionary, but I could not leave our little flock. Yet, because some of us did stay in Assisi, hundreds of others were able to go out and carry the message of Christ to the whole world.

I came to understand, therefore, that all organization is not bad. It is organization that keeps a good idea going, that helps pool resources and energies. But we must not let organization take the place of personal commitment to God; we must have both. The church is the organized body of Christ.

The final thing I would like to share with you is my discovery that if we approach life with love, we find God. All my life I have loved nature: the sweetness of new-mown fields, the whispering of wind in the trees, the warmth of sun, the light of the moon, the refreshment of cooling rivers, and all of these things have led me to the Creator whose handiwork they are.

It is the same with the love of animals. We built nests in our church yard for the doves, and they would light upon us just as God's spirit came upon our Lord. I once let a rabbit out of a trap and it followed me for a day. I let a fish go from a hook and it stayed by our boat all afternoon. I tamed a wolf once by showing him he had nothing to fear. All these things show me that we are bound together with all creation by ties of love.

I have found this to be especially true with regard to people. I learned to love the leper as a child of God and in so doing I found my own freedom to be a child of God. I have seen enemies turned into friends when reminded of God's forgiveness of all of us. I have seen the rich released from captivity to their wealth by the awareness of the needs of others.

It is true, whatever our circumstance, that when we approach life with love, we find God. I have been in love with Lady Poverty and it has been treasure enough. I have experienced severe illness, but the love of God was my consolation. I was willing to suffer with Jesus Christ, and God has exalted my spirit.

For all these reasons I call upon you and all creation to praise the Lord, thanking God for all God's goodness. For God is love, and he has so made the world that whenever we approach life with love, we find God, and in finding God, we find our own contentment.

Chapter Ten

Often, those remembered as heroes by the church have been clergy. Since the vast majority of constituents in the church are laity, it is meaningful for them to see that many of the persons who kept their integrity in times of great difficulty have been laypersons. Thomas More was a person of strong faith who did not give up his principles when they became inconvenient. He was cautious, not bold, but when circumstances required that he give up his integrity or his life, he found the courage to maintain his integrity. People facing difficult choices today need to know that others have faced great challenges and remained faithful to what they believed.

I wanted to prepare a message for Reformation Sunday. After reading several books on Thomas More, I developed a story line that I thought would help the congregation understand how the events of history have impacted and changed the church. Telling it from the perspective of an involved participant would keep it from being simply a history lesson. Having a devout Roman Catholic tell of events leading to the establishment of Protestantism in England would lead to a greater appreciation of our shared heritage.

The proposition that guided the development of the sermon was as follows: "As we learn about one who was faithful to his convictions, we are helped to be faithful to our convictions." I decided that I would represent More as speaking in his prison cell just before being taken to his execution. Since many in the congregation would not know for sure what finally happened to More, I had the following statement printed in the worship folder under the sermon title: "Thomas More was beheaded on July 6, 1535. On the scaffold he said, 'I die the king's good servant, but God's first.' "

A Man Of Integrity

Philippians 4:4-9

"It is better to take refuge in the Lord than to put confidence in princes." So says the Psalmist. And I have found it so in my own life. I had known it from the beginning of my career, but the events of history made it impossible for me to keep aloof from the influence of princes. So it is that you see me now, bereft of family, career, titles, wealth — and soon to be bereft of my head, for tomorrow the headsman will have that — and I am left only with the temporary use of this prison cell, and with my integrity. Like the Apostle Paul, I know what it is to abound, and also what it is to be abased. May God continue to give me the strength I need for one more day to meet the great challenge that still lies ahead.

My name is Thomas More, sometime lord chancellor, that is, prime minister, of all England, and close confidant of my prince, King Henry VIII. How my star has fallen since those days — and all for conscience sake. Let me tell you about it.

I was born in London in 1478. At the age of fourteen I was sent to Canterbury College, Oxford, where I would have been happy to continue in the scholarly and contemplative life of the clergy, but my father wanted me to become a lawyer and enrolled me instead in the study of the law. I eventually concluded that it was my calling to be a layman rather than a priest, and I embraced the law, though I have always preferred the simplicity of dress, food, and drink I experienced among the monks.

Following my entrance into the practice of law, I turned to public affairs and was elected to the House of Commons at the age of 24. Life was pleasant for me. I married Jane Colt, who bore me four children in five years. My practice was prospering. I was appointed to be undersheriff of London, which was a judgeship.

When my wife died suddenly, I quickly married a widow with children of her own, for I needed someone to manage the household, and our families were happily merged. Worship was most important to me. We observed morning and evening prayers, we listened to the Scriptures being read at meal time, and we attended mass daily. We felt that our blessings were to be shared, so we built a house for the poor which was cared for by the whole family. While we were a pious family, our house was filled with mirth and games and plays and the learning of music, which was shared by the whole household. I lamented that I did not have the time to be a real scholar, but as a family man, it was important that I spend time with the family.

In 1509, Henry VII died, and his son, Henry VIII, was crowned king. We who were educated looked forward to his reign, for the new king was educated in Latin, theology, philosophy, science, and letters. He was a bonnie prince. We believed that the tyranny we had experienced under the former king was over. With such an enlightened prince coming to the throne, we felt there would be an improvement in the lot of the common man. Alas, we did not understand the corrupting nature of power.

A constellation of circumstances was already taking shape that none of us had the ability to foresee, but which would have a profound effect on England, the Church, and ourselves. Before ascending the throne, Henry had married a Spanish princess, Catherine of Aragon. She had previously been married to Henry's brother, Arthur, but Arthur had died before the marriage was consummated. Normally the Church did not allow a person to marry his brother's wife, but since the marriage had not been consummated, the pope gave a dispensation, allowing Henry to marry her. Some questioned the validity of the dispensation, including the archbishop of Canterbury.

As Henry assumed the crown, he turned often for advice to Thomas Wolsey, an ambitious man I had known from my time at Oxford. Wolsey encouraged Henry to make war on France and Scotland, for he hoped to advance his own cause in the settlements. Somehow, I caught Wolsey's attention and he had me appointed to a diplomatic delegation to Flanders. I was away for six months, which greatly affected the income of my law practice. During that time I developed ideas for a book about the kinds of changes that would be necessary in society to bring about the ideal commonwealth. It was about a society ruled by reason. It was also a protest against social injustice. I called the book *Utopia*. It was published in 1516.

In 1515, Thomas Wolsey was made a cardinal in the Church. That same year Henry made him lord chancellor of England. Henry wanted to put me on the royal payroll because of my service in Flanders. I declined because I felt it would compromise my position as a judge. In 1516, a daughter, Mary Tudor, was born to Henry and the queen, Catherine. The king was pleased to have an heir, but mentioned privately that he *really* needed a son.

On May Day, 1517, an angry crowd was beginning to riot in London over social conditions. I spoke to them and, as a consequence, what could have been a revolution was averted. Wolsey was convinced that the king needed my services and insisted that I enter the royal payroll as the king's counselor. I acquiesced and entered into the life at court. All the while the king was learning statecraft from his lord chancellor, Wolsey, who taught him to be ruthless in the exercise of power. One of England's leading nobles was jailed for treason, found guilty, and executed. I marked well how the king managed to accomplish his will within the law but to use the law to his advantage. It would not be healthy to incur the wrath of the king.

I now became familiar to the king and queen. I was frequently invited for conversation with them, but, as they might request my presence at any time, day or night, I feigned dullness in conversation so they would call on me less, and I could spend time with my family, which was my personal priority. Even so, the king and I worked together frequently on matters of state, and we came to like each other. I worked with the king to seek an alliance with France, and for my services the king made me a knight and elevated me to the office of sub-treasurer of the exchequer. The king treated me as a close friend, occasionally even coming to my home unannounced for meals. My son-in-law, William Roper, was much impressed by this friendship, but remembering the noble who had been executed, I pointed out to him that if my head would bring the king a castle in France, the king would be quick to give it.

For his part, Wolsey, who had brought me into such familiarity with the king, was becoming increasingly isolated in his grandeur.

He was lord chancellor of England, cardinal of the Holy Roman Church, and supreme ecclesiastical authority in England. The opulence in which he lived exceeded that of the king. There was no end to his avarice and thirst for power.

Events, seemingly disconnected, continued to weave a web that would eventually change England and the Church, and in the process, bring me to my present circumstances. As is often the case with royalty, the king dallied with many women at court. One of the ladies in waiting, Mary Boleyn, eventually became his mistress. Her younger sister, Anne, observed that this brought nothing to Mary, and concluded that if she ever had the interest of the king, she would arrange things differently. Anne became involved in a romance with a young noble, and Wolsey sent her off to the country to get over it. For this, Anne developed a hatred of Wolsey.

Henry continued to have problems with the king of Spain, who was also the emperor of the Holy Roman Empire, and nephew of the queen.

Henry was also heard to say how important it was for him to have a son, but he feared that Catherine was now past child-bearing age.

By this time some of the writings of Martin Luther were coming to us in England. I wrote numerous papers against this heresy and in defense of our Holy Catholic faith. The king did likewise, writing a treatise in support of the papacy. He also had books by Luther burned publicly. For this the pope bestowed on Henry the title, "Defender of the Faith," a title which delighted Henry and added to his self-understanding as a person significant in the life of the Church.

The king directed Wolsey to pursue further negotiations with France, and he told Wolsey to include me in the negotiations. Negotiations continued to move along well. Indeed, the king was so satisfied that he made me chancellor of the Duchy of Lancaster.

The king was pleased with everything but his marriage. He began to mutter aloud that perhaps his marriage to Catherine was flawed. Though he had received a papal dispensation to marry his brother's wife, he now wondered if the papacy had had all the facts. Wolsey fanned the flames of Henry's distress as he was now favorable to the idea of having Henry free to marry a French princess, thereby sealing an alliance with France and giving Wolsey even more influence.

In the meantime, Anne Boleyn had returned from the country and had managed to capture the attention of the king. Not wanting to end up as a discarded mistress, as her sister had, Anne continued to tantalize the king for years, as the king became ever more disenchanted with his marriage. In 1527, Wolsey decided to act on the king's behalf by setting up a trial that would look into what was now called the king's illegitimate marriage. Wolsey even made arrangements to have Henry marry a French princess when Henry would be free, not realizing Henry's interest in Anne — and Anne's interest in being queen — a fatal blunder for Wolsey. Wolsey asked the pope to grant Henry an annulment, but the Pope continued to put off a decision, because the king of Spain, Catherine's nephew, opposed it.

When I returned to England in 1527, the king summoned me to his chambers, presented his case, and asked for my opinion. I protested that it was a theological matter, and therefore beyond my field. Though he often asked, I never gave my opinion to him or to anyone. Henry asked the pope for a dispensation allowing him to marry without settling the annulment issue. When nothing happened on that score, the king summoned Wolsey to explain why Henry was getting no satisfaction. Anne was present and openly humiliated Wolsey, apparently with Henry's permission, showing who now had the king's favor.

A trial was eventually held. It proceeded with intentional slowness, came to no conclusion, and was eventually transferred to Rome, much to the anger of Henry and Anne. At issue was the interpretation of a text in the Old Testament book of Leviticus which stated that a man must not lie with a brother's wife and that as punishment they shall be childless. Henry contended that God was not blessing his marriage with a son because he was wrongly married to his brother's wife. Since the matter involved biblical interpretation, one of Henry's advisors suggested that the matter be decided by the biblical faculties of the European universities. The king agreed.

Wolsey was now clearly out of favor for having been unable to require the pope to act on Henry's request. The king stripped Wolsey of his chancellorship and his wealth and banished him to his country home. Soon thereafter he was accused of treason and arrested. He did not come to trial, for he became ill and died on the trip to London.

Henry then appointed me to the office of lord chancellor in 1527. I tried to avoid entanglement in the king's domestic problems, and instead spent my time and energy hearing cases, making judgments, and reforming the English court system. The opinions from the universities were beginning to come in, but they were inconclusive. Those faculties subsidized by Henry voted in his favor. Those subsidized by the king of Spain voted against Henry. Once again Henry appealed to the pope to grant him an annulment, but still the pope procrastinated and at the same time gave orders that no clergy could marry Henry while the case was under review.

Henry was at the end of his patience. He needed to have a church in which he could accomplish what he wanted to accomplish, so he called a convocation of English clergy. When they were assembled, he advised them that they were all suspected of disloyalty because they had taken a vow to obey the pope. They were all accused of treason. The only way the charges would be dropped would be for the clergy to accept Henry as the supreme head of the Church in England. Recognizing what had happened to others who frustrated the king, the clergy agreed to Henry's terms.

The king moved quickly now to fulfill his wishes and sever ties with the Church at Rome. In July, 1530, he left his wife and installed Anne Boleyn in Catherine's apartments. He required the House of Commons to withhold revenue that was to have been sent by the Church to Rome. Through threat of punishment, on May 15, 1532, he required the clergy to sign a document known as the Submission of the Clergy. Henry had set himself up to be the head of the Church of England.

The next day I surrendered my credentials and resigned as lord chancellor. I pleaded ill health, but actually I could no longer serve a government that was interfering with the Church. I said nothing that was critical of the king, but I was aware that silence alone would not satisfy the king. My own wealth had been spent in public office, my resignation prevented me from receiving a pension, and I felt it inappropriate to practice law, having been lord chancellor. I took to writing, but mostly religious tracts, criticizing the Lutheran heresy and defending the clergy, but there was not much money in it. I advised my family that we needed to be prepared to live in austerity. I thought it appropriate also to acquaint my family with the lives of the martyrs, those who had died for what they believed. They needed to be prepared for what might come.

Henry saw to it that one of his supporters was elected archbishop of Canterbury, the highest office in the English Church. Parliament then passed a bill giving the archbishop the authority to settle the case of the king's divorce. The archbishop announced that Henry's marriage to Catherine had been no marriage, and that her daughter, Mary, was therefore illegitimate. Catherine was maintained in seclusion. In January, 1535, Henry secretly married Anne, who presented him with a daughter, Elizabeth.

Anne's coronation as queen was to be splendid. I was urged to be present, but I declined, pleading poverty. The king was offended by my absence and by my failure to speak out in favor of his actions. Subsequently, numerous charges were brought against me, but each time, they were dismissed for lack of evidence. Some officials promised me favors if I would simply approve the king's divorce and acknowledge him to be head of the Church of England. That failing, they reminded me that the indignation of a prince means death. I needed no reminder. I was sure that the king would not let the matter lie.

In 1534, a commission was set up whose purpose it was to extract an oath of obedience from any they chose to examine. Those examined were required to acknowledge Henry to be the head of the Church of England and thereby renounce all obedience to the pope. I was eventually summoned and required to subscribe to the king's supremacy over the Church. If I refused, I knew that death was certain and that my family would suffer. My family prevailed upon me to give in, pointing out that all the bishops had done so and gone free. I was imprisoned in the Tower while the commission waited for my answer. The imprisonment became increasingly severe, and I was informed of the agonizing deaths of those who refused to take the oath. I was denied access to my books, to writing materials, and eventually to my family.

Thus far I had not denied the king's supremacy; I had simply not taken the oath. To be strictly legal, the court would need evidence that I denied Henry's supremacy. I felt that the oath was a two-edged sword: if I should speak against it, I would procure the death of my body; if I should consent to it, I would procure the death of my soul.

Since I failed to take the oath, I was finally taken to trial just a few days ago. I was accused of four offenses: giving a malicious opinion of the king's marriage; encouraging a priest to resist the oath of supremacy; refusing to acknowledge the king's supremacy; denying the king's supremacy and in so doing denying the king's royal authority. I was told that the king was merciful. If I would change my opinion, I would obtain pardon. I indicated that none of the charges was true, for I had never opened my conscience to anyone on these matters. One fellow, however, eager to advance himself with the king, perjured himself, saying that I had said that Parliament could not make the king the supreme head of the Church. The jury met for fifteen minutes, found me guilty, and sentenced me to death. I concluded that it was not for the supremacy that my life was being sought, but for my failure to approve the king's second marriage. I was marched back to the Tower of London where my dear daughter, Meg, was waiting. She kissed me, but could not speak.

What can I say about all of this? I am not an heroic person. I have not sought death or been indifferent to the dangers. I have not sought to incur the wrath of the king by openly challenging him. What the king would do in his personal life was the king's business, not mine. But if we are to have a civilized society, a person must not be forced to violate conscience under threat of death. What I am doing in refusing to take an oath regarding the king's supremacy in the Church is a matter of conscience. The king has sought to bend me to his will. I am the king's subject, but I am God's subject first. That priority is something each of us must decide for ourself.

Chapter Eleven

Most informed church people of my generation have at least heard of Albert Schweitzer. They know that he was a doctor who served in Africa. They may not know of him as a theologian, philosopher, or as a musician. I wanted the members of my congregation to become better acquainted with him and his work so that they would have a greater appreciation for foreign missionaries and also be challenged to examine how they might use their own gifts.

As I read several books by and about Schweitzer, it became apparent that I could not include everything about the man in the time allotted for a sermon. I would have to be selective. I decided to focus on his life up to the end of World War I. This would help people to see how his life and thought developed, and still provide him sufficient opportunity to speak about his experiences in Africa. The one-sentence summary that guided the development of this sermon is as follows: "Albert Schweitzer's life and thought challenge us to cultivate our gifts, to live boldly for God, and to have reverence for life."

A Reverence For Life

I was sitting on the deck of a barge, lost in thought as we crept slowly upstream on one of those long African errands of mercy. I was struggling to find that elementary and universal conception of the ethical life which I had not discovered in any philosophy. I had covered page after page of my notebook with disconnected sentences, merely to keep myself concentrated on the problem.

Late on the third day, at the very moment when, at sunset, we were making our way through a herd of hippopotamuses, there flashed upon my mind unforeseen and unsought, the phrase, "Reverence for Life." The iron door had yielded; the path through the thicket had become visible. I had found my way to the idea in which world-affirmation, life-affirmation, and ethics are contained side by side. In that simple phrase I was able to crystallize the thought which had motivated much of my life and conduct, and discovered what was, for me, the fundamental principle of morality, namely, that good consists in maintaining, assisting, and enhancing life, and that to destroy, to harm, or to hinder life is evil. It was such a thought, perhaps intuited, but heretofore unarticulated, which had brought me to where I was, a jungle doctor serving my brothers and sisters at the edge of the forest primeval in French Equatorial Africa.

My name is Albert Schweitzer. I would like to share with you some of the thoughts and experiences which molded my life in the hope that what I discovered might be helpful to you as you search for the meaning of life.

To be sure, my upbringing contributed mightily to anything I was to make of myself. I was born in Kayserberg, Upper Alsace, which was then German, in January, 1875. My father was a pastor in the Evangelical Church, and my mother was daughter of a pastor, so my religious heritage was assured. We soon moved to the village of Gunsbach, which is where I grew up. My father began training me on the piano when I was five. I began to play the organ when I was eight, and I took the place of the Gunsbach organist for a while when I was nine. The organ was my first love, a love that was to last all my life. When I went away to high school I lived with my godfather, who was an organist, and he gave me lessons.

Even in my early years I was developing an appreciation for all living things. I can remember as a pre-school child that it wasn't quite clear to me why my evening prayers should only be for human beings. After my mother had prayed with me and turned out the lights I used to pray silently, "O, heavenly Father, protect and bless all things that have breath; guard them from all evil and let them sleep in peace."

On another occasion, when I was eight, a friend and I had made slingshots. "Let's go and shoot some birds," he said. It was a terrible proposal to me, but I did not dare refuse for fear he would laugh at me. Just as we took aim at some birds, a church bell began to ring and frightened the birds away. I remember how grateful I was. Now, when I hear the church bells, they remind me, "Thou shalt not kill."

In 1893, I entered the University of Strasbourg and my academic training began in earnest. I studied theology, philosophy, and music theory. In preparation for my Ph.D., I studied also in Paris and Berlin. I received my degree in 1899, writing a doctoral dissertation on the philosophy of Kant. I was now prepared to teach, but my interest was theology.

I passed the first exams in theology and became assistant pastor at a church in Strasbourg. I came to some conclusions about Jesus which disagreed with the opinions of orthodox Christianity, but I nevertheless obtained my theological degree, was ordained in the ministry, became a university instructor and the principal of a theological seminary.

All the while I was also pursuing my organ studies. I had opportunity to travel widely as a concert organist, and in this interval I became well acquainted with the organ music of Bach. I published a book on Bach and became something of an authority on his life and his music, so that I was often invited to speak on Bach and to interpret his music throughout Europe. Not only was I interested in *playing* the organ, I was interested in what went on inside. Frequently, when I was to play at a concert I would find that some of the great old organs had not been kept up, so it was necessary to get in and work on them. I wrote an extensive essay on organs and organ building, urging that old organs be saved and restored rather than replaced by newer factory-built instruments. Thereafter, I received hundreds of letters asking for advice and design with regard to organ building and repair, and I was able to design many.

When I began lecturing in theology at the University in 1902, there were those who opposed my appointment. Some faculty members felt that what I had to say about Jesus would confuse the students. Still, I was hired. In 1906, I published a book titled *The Quest For The Historical Jesus*. My conclusion was that Jesus had mistakenly expected the end of the world in his lifetime. The suggestion that Jesus could have been mistaken about anything, of course, was an affront to the cherished beliefs of the time. Personally, I felt no less constrained to follow Jesus, and I maintained that we are still called to loyalty and commitment to him, though we must learn for our own time how that loyalty is to be expressed.

These, as you may well imagine, were great days for me. I had achieved everything I had ever wanted. Recognition as a philosopher, a theologian, a musician. But I was also aware of an obligation. I had recognized, even as a youngster, how happy and blessed I was in contrast with others in the world who could not enjoy life: I had nourishing food when others did not; I had shoes when others did not. As early as age 21 I decided that I must make some return for the happiness I knew. I resolved to spend my time till age thirty living for science and art, and then from that time on I would devote myself to the service of humanity.

My most life-altering decision came as I approached my thirtieth year. Through much of my life I had attempted to deal with those words of Jesus, "He who would save his life must be prepared to lose it." In 1904, I chanced to read an article describing the great need for medical help in French Equatorial Africa, an area under the sponsorship of the Parisian Missionary Society. Quietly, without consulting family or friends, I decided to respond. Friends and family were distressed when I told them. They felt I would be burying the talent entrusted to me. They felt it was a great waste to begin to prepare for a new field at the age of thirty. They probed for reasons: disappointment in my career; perhaps a thwarted romance? But as I've said, it was a simple attempt to be obedient to the command of Jesus, my Lord; and the prospect made me enormously happy.

I embarked on my medical studies in 1905, at the age of thirty. They occupied much of my time for the next seven years. During this time I gave up my principalship, though I continued to teach and to preach. I gave more organ concerts because my reputation as an interpreter of Bach had grown, and because I needed the income to support me in my studies. I continued writing in the areas of philosophy, theology, and music, in which I had developed a considerable following.

All this while, however, there was some doubt whether the Parisian Missionary Society would even accept me. They had an orthodox zeal for saving souls. My religious views were unorthodox, and quite well known. I passed the medical exams in 1911 and wrote a dissertation for my MD degree on the subject of Jesus' mental health. While I concluded that Jesus' estimate of himself was quite in accord with the expectations of his time, simply subjecting Jesus to a psychological analysis was upsetting to conservative Christians.

The time came when I had to give up my teaching and preaching positions as I set out for Paris to study tropical medicine. Knowing that there were some orthodox members of the missionary board who could not in good conscience support someone with my views, I proposed to the society that I would go out at my own expense and secure my own support, if they would allow me to serve from their central mission station at Lambarene. Many were delighted, but some wanted to examine my beliefs. I refused on the basis that when Jesus called his disciples he required nothing of them but the willingness to follow. I did offer to visit each member separately for a private conversation. Some feared that I might choose to preach or confuse the missionaries. I indicated that I would avoid this, and they accepted my offer.

Now came the time of preparing to go. I gave concerts and lectures to finance the work. I had to ask friends to support the project, and this was humiliating. Up to this time I had been self-supporting, now I was to serve with the help of others. Eventually,

I had enough for the necessary supplies and to run the hospital for a year. At this time, at the age of 37, I married Helen Bresslau. She was a nurse; she would be of great help in the running of a hospital.

Africa was an enormous challenge. When we arrived in 1913, there were no medical buildings. We set up our work in a chicken house. My wife was nurse and administrator. Joseph, a native, was cook, attendant, interpreter, and adviser. At once we had to find accommodations for forty patients a day and their companions.

How incredible was our opportunity! A poor moaning creature might be brought to me in great pain. I would lay my hand on his forehead and tell him that in an hour's time he would have an operation that would remove the pain. He is scarcely awake after the operation and cries for joy, "I have no more pain!" His hand feels for mine and will not let go. Then I tell him and the others who are with him that it is the Lord Jesus who has told the doctor and his wife to come to Africa. I tell him about the white people in Europe who give money so that Africans may be made well; and we, black and white, sit side by side and feel that we know by experience the meaning of Jesus' words, "All of you are brothers."

I did not discuss doctrine with the missionaries, only how to increase practical Christianity among the natives. Eventually, however, I was invited to preach, and was released from my promise to the mission society. Some of the native pastors, trained by the missionaries, did protest my participation in their theological discussions, however, because, they said, I was a doctor and not a theologian as they were.

Even in Africa I had time for my music. At night I would work on further editions of Bach's music. To keep up my organ skills, the Bach Society had presented me with a piano built for the tropics and with a pedal attachment to simulate the footwork of an organ. I would work on one piece at a time, perfecting it for the day I would again be able to play the organ.

In 1914, war broke out. As we were Germans in a French colony, we were placed under house arrest, and for a time, prohibited even from the practice of medicine. When the natives heard about war in Europe, they felt it was senseless, for white men didn't even eat those they killed.

I, too, was questioning the progress of civilization. The only way out of chaos would be for civilization to adopt an attitude toward life built on ethical ideals. But what is that ethical foundation? It was this thought that continued to trouble me when I was released from house arrest and permitted to resume my medical duties.

Then came the trip up river, which I mentioned at the outset. The phrase "reverence for life" came to my mind. I came to see that the most immediate fact of our consciousness is the assertion, "I am life that wills to live." What is good, then, is what preserves life, promotes life, develops it to its fullest. And evil is what destroys life, injures life, represses development. And these ethical values relate to *all* life, not just to humans. This was the truth I had intuited as a child when my conscience resisted shooting birds.

Unfortunately, contempt for life characterizes our age. We wage wars, which no one wins, and bring suffering and death to millions of humans and animals, because we do not possess reverence for life. And because we do not possess it, everyone is afraid of everyone else. There is no remedy for our situation apart from reverence for life. I have come to the conviction that people are ethical only when life, as such, is sacred to them — the life of plants and animals, as well as the life of human beings, and when they demonstrate that ethic by devoting themselves helpfully to all life that is in need of help. Sometimes we are forced to choose which forms of life, or even which individuals, are to be saved or destroyed, but the principle of maintaining and furthering all life is, nevertheless, valid. The ethical person destroys life only from necessity, never from thoughtlessness, and always with a profound sense of regret.

I suppose we have come full circle, at least for today. I began with how the concept of reverence for life came to me, and I have now developed what it means.

Perhaps it remains to recount briefly subsequent events of my life. We were eventually sent to France, and then repatriated to Germany in a prisoner exchange. When the war was over, I again had opportunity to lecture and to play the organ in concert, in order to accumulate money for our return to Africa. Thereafter, for decades, I would frequently return to Europe for lecture and concert tours, acquiring the funds which were so necessary for the operation of our hospital in Lambarene. I continued to write of our experiences in Africa, and of the thoughts which those experiences generated. Therefore, our work was brought to the attention of people around the world, and people everywhere contributed to the work. Consequently, our hospital became an expression of world-wide Christian compassion.

There are several thoughts I would like to leave with you that come out of my experience. For one thing, if God has given you a talent, cultivate it. Who knows what you may be able to do with it. Who would have thought that organ concerts, which brought so much joy of accomplishment to me, would have been turned into medicine and medical services for the needy of Africa?

Secondly, let me urge you to attempt bold things. Most of us have far more gifts than we give ourselves credit for. God has not been stingy in what he has provided; it is we who are stingy when we refuse to develop the gifts that have been given.

And finally, have reverence for life. If people will only begin to think about the mystery of their lives, and the links which connect them with the life that fills the world, they cannot help but experience a reverence for life and a feeling of oneness with all that lives. It is that sense of oneness that makes us moral, that gives us a sense of responsibility, not only for our human family, but for all God's creatures, and for the planet, which is our shared home. What each individual has to contribute is her or his own secret. But we all need to learn that our existence only attains its true value when we have experienced the truth of Jesus' declaration: "The one who loses his life for my sake will find it."

Chapter Twelve

So much of what we hear about politicians and world leaders causes us to question whether there are any who are guided by religious convictions. I was delighted to read Dag Hammarskjold's book *Markings* and to find revealed there a man whose exceptional faith and piety guided and strengthened him as he gave leadership to the United Nations. Many people of my generation would know of him as a world leader, but would be unacquainted with him as a man of Christian convictions. They would be encouraged to hear of his struggle for faith and his search for divine guidance.

This sermon was prepared for delivery on World Order Sunday, a time when my denomination focuses on issues of peace and justice. My objective in the sermon was to show, through the experiences of Dag Hammarskjold, how faith develops, matures, and influences the one who possesses it. For those persons who might not be aware of the circumstances of Hammarskjold's death, I had the following statement printed under the sermon title in the worship folder: "Dag Hammarskjold died in a mysterious plane crash in Congo on September 17, 1961, while on a mission seeking to bring peace to a troubled land."

Trail Markers

In 1953, not long after I had come to New York to be inducted as secretary-general of the United Nations, I was asked to appear on a radio program with Edward R. Murrow. He wanted me to speak about what I believed. I wrote a brief statement which I called "Old Creeds in a New World." In that statement I laid out several of the things that I was aware of which had brought me to that point. I'd like to share with you some of the trail markers that have guided me on the journey of faith. While the experiences of each individual are unique, I think that we can derive strength for our own pilgrimage by hearing how others have been helped.

In case you don't know, my name is Dag Hammarskjold. I call what I have to say "trail markers" because I see the quest of each of us as a climb toward our destiny, toward God. Mountain climbing is my favorite recreation. In my native land of Sweden, mountain climbing doesn't so much call for skill as for endurance. Sometimes, as we climb or hike, we lay down trail markers so that we can tell the way we have come and where we have been. Through much of my life I have kept a journal of my most private thoughts, a journal that I call "Trail Markers," or "Markings" if you will, because those recorded thoughts help me to see where I have been. I have referred to them often in preparing these thoughts to be shared with you.

Among those things which have shaped my faith, I referred in my talk for Mr. Murrow to the early influences of home and childhood. I was born in Jonkoping, Sweden, in 1905. My father was governor of the Uppsala Province for almost 25 years, except for a three-year interval when he was prime minister of Sweden, so almost all of my childhood was spent in the Governor's Castle. As a child I enjoyed crawling through the labyrinthine passages of the old castle. The archbishop of Sweden and his family lived in the archbishop's palace just down the hill from us, so our families were good friends. From my earliest years my father impressed upon me a belief that no life is more satisfactory than one of selfless service to one's country or to humanity. Such service, he pointed out, would require a sacrifice of all personal interests, but for three centuries our family had provided that kind of service to Sweden.

While my father was a rather stern and formal Lutheran, my mother was a warm and generous lady who repeatedly impressed on me that all people are equals as God's children, and that they should be met and treated by us as our masters in God. What I learned from my parents was not so much a formal theology of traditional Christian teaching, but an active compassion toward all in need and a compelling sense of duty.

I entered Uppsala University at the age of seventeen and completed my Bachelor of Arts degree in two years. Subsequently, I was to take a degree in law, and to earn my doctorate in Economics.

I have always enjoyed mountaineering. I feel it gives one character to be out in nature, and being alone in nature has often given me a renewal of spirit.

By disposition I have always been a shy person, reserved, uncommunicative, solitary. This has troubled me greatly. Though others have not known it, I have been lonely to the point of despair. Unable to share my innermost thoughts with others, I started to write them down in my journal when I was twenty. Thoughts of death, guilt, and the meaninglessness of life frequently disturbed me. The sense of duty, moral obligation, and the call to public service were heavy burdens and I often fought against them inwardly. Like so many Swedes, I sometimes entertained thoughts of suicide, yet no one knew of my inner struggle. I believe that companions and colleagues alike have found me to be pleasant and apparently happy. Yet the call to duty, learned from my parents, was for many years both my cross and my strength.

Strangely enough, the higher my career ascended, the deeper my spirit descended. I became secretary to the Royal Commission on Unemployment during the Depression, then the under-secretary in the Ministry of Finance, and eventually, chairman of the Bank of Sweden. I created a pattern of total dedication to my work which provided no place for marriage or family obligations. As my companions married, they were less available for late night talks, early morning walks, weekend hikes; as a consequence, my sense of loneliness increased. I moved to the Foreign Ministry in 1946, eventually becoming the vice-minister of foreign affairs. I was at the pinnacle of civic life in Sweden and seen by all as an outstanding success.

Yet, in spite of this, I was experiencing an inner despondency that bordered on despair. I suffered from a solitariness that I could not overcome, an incurable loneliness of the soul from which I felt there would be no release. I needed something to live for, or if necessary, something great enough to die for. It occurred to me that death might be the only cure, but sometimes I wondered if loneliness were an obligatory part of the way of service which I had chosen. I could not ask a woman to share my life with me, for she would be left alone much of the time, as my mother had been left alone so much because of my father's work. I felt like a Catholic priest who had renounced marriage in order to give his love to all people.

In my despair, I was led to meditate on the life of Jesus. I had begun to read Albert Schweitzer's great book, *The Quest For The Historical Jesus*. In its pages I encountered Jesus approaching his end as a committed young man who was alone as he confronted his final destiny. Here was a man who touched my condition, alone but courageous. And Schweitzer had been touched by him too, so much that he willingly gave up all to follow Jesus in humble service. I had already heard the call of duty and service from my parents, but I didn't know *why* I was supposed to respond. I wanted something to live for, something great enough to die for, but I had not yet discovered it.

I had reached a turning point in my life. I had been immersing myself in the writings of certain early Christian mystics, people like Meister Eckhart, Saint John of the Cross, Thomas a Kempis, Pascal. These people had discovered God as a living reality; indeed, they came to believe that God lived in them and used them in advancing his great purposes. They surrendered themselves and found self-realization. They found strength to say, "Yes," to the needs of their neighbors and, "Yes," to every fate life had in store for them when they followed the call of duty. I had always followed the call of duty, but I had never made it my conscious choice.

I had been afraid of what it might mean and where it might lead, and that made me hold something back.

On New Years Day, 1952, I determined to hold back no longer. Suddenly, everything broke out of me in glorious affirmation. I was prepared to say, "Yes," to whatever came my way; to live affirmatively regardless of the cost. In that act of daring to say, "Yes," I found meaning for my life and for all things in which I would become involved. I had asked for meaning: now I found it. I am not sure what the question was, but I am confident that in that moment I said, "Yes," to God, and from that moment I was certain that existence is meaningful and that my life had a goal. Since that moment I have come to understand what Jesus meant when he told his disciples not to look back and not to be anxious about tomorrow. I had found God, or been found by him, and I was prepared to follow wherever the Way would lead.

Shortly thereafter I was nominated to become secretary-general of the United Nations, a position which my predecessor, Trygve Lie, warned me was the most impossible job in the world. My induction was to take place around Easter week of 1953. As I considered this event in my own life, I was also meditating on the last week of Jesus' life before the crucifixion. I began to understand that one who surrenders to God's will may find that it leads to a cross, even if, temporarily, it leads to exaltation, just as Jesus discovered that the triumphal entry into Jerusalem was, nevertheless, the way to the cross. My vocation was being defined not *by* me, but *for* me. It was clear that God had a use for me, whether it happened to suit me at the moment or not. Jesus became for me the one who pursued the human destiny God had ordained for him to its bitter and seemingly disastrous end. He enjoined all who would follow him to do likewise, for he said, "If anyone would come after me, let him deny himself, take up his cross, and follow." At every moment Jesus is dying in someone who has followed the trail markers of love and patience, righteousness and humility, faith, courage, and stillness to the end. I had been chosen, as have all followers of Jesus.

It is the knowledge that I have been called to this place which has made it possible for me to offer my service to the

United Nations. The crises have been endless. In 1954 China threatened to try twelve captured American airmen as spies. As I flew to Peking in an attempt to resolve the crisis, I felt helpless until I reflected on the words of Psalm 139: "If I ascend to heaven thou art there. If I make my bed in Sheol, thou art there." God was with me. The airmen were released. I received much praise, but I received it in shame mixed with gratitude, for I realized that I was but an instrument in the hands of God.

There were crises in the Middle East — Suez and Lebanon — in South East Asia, in South Africa, and a crisis in which Nikita Krushchev demonstrated his hostility by thumping his desk and insisting that the office of secretary-general be dissolved because, he said, "The Soviet Union does not trust Dag Hammarskjold." In spite of such difficulties I was proposed for a second five-year term in 1957 and confirmed. Why would one accept it? I came to the conclusion that one has never done enough so long as one still has something of value to contribute. I had said, "Yes," to God, "Yes," to my destiny, "Yes," to myself. I would not back away.

Since my second induction as secretary-general, my faith has been maturing. What started out as duty that led me through Jesus to God, now became an awareness of God through Jesus that led to a new and fulfilling sense of duty. There were fewer thoughts now of loneliness, death, and sacrifice. I have come to see that my loneliness has made it easier to give myself to God's purposes and to serve others. I have come to see that the Way has chosen me, and I must follow it wherever it leads. The example of Jesus has strengthened my conviction that the road of possibility might lead to the cross. As it was with Jesus on Palm Sunday, I have come to see that the Way leads to a triumph which is a catastrophe, and to a catastrophe which is a triumph. As I face whatever the future holds for me, I am confident that the God who may abase me for his purpose, also has the power to raise me up. I am ready, come what may — the trail markers are in place. I will not lose my way.